Pioneer,
Polygamist,
Politician

Pioneer, Polygamist, Politician

The Life of Dr. Martha Hughes Cannon

Mari Graña

TWODOT®

GUILFORD, CONNECTICUT
HELENA, MONTANA
AN IMPRINT OF THE GLOBE PEQUOT PRESS

Project editor: Jessica Haberman
Text design: Sheryl P. Kober
Layout: Sue Murray

Graña, Mari, 1936-
Pioneer, polygamist, politician: the life of Dr. Martha Hughes
Cannon / Mari Graña.
p. cm.
Includes bibliographical references.
ISBN 978-0-7627-5272-0
1. Cannon, Martha Hughes. 2. Mormons–Utah—Biography. 3.
Utah–Biography. 4. Physicians–Utah—Biography. 5. Polygamy–
Utah. 6. Legislators–Utah—Biography. 7. Utah. Legislature.
Senate–Biography. 8. Utah–Politics and government-20th century.
I. Title.
BX8695.C26G73 2009
289.3092—dc22
[B]
2009002897

Printed in the United States of America
10 9 8 7 6 5 4 3 2 1

For
SHARRON WELSH,
the best of research associates

Martha Hughes Cannon, ca. 1880

Contents

Introduction

The Church of Jesus Christ of Latter-day Saints (LDS Church) was established in western New York State by Joseph Smith Jr. at the time of America's "Second Great Awakening," a period of religious fervor in the country that resulted in the development of several offshoots of established Christian groups. Most of these have died out, but over the years the LDS Church has survived to become extremely successful, both in its number of members and as an economic entity.

A young teenager, Joseph Smith, is said to have found and translated through divine guidance a text written on certain gold plates. The text recorded a history of ancient America reaching back as far as 2200 BCE and included the record of a visit to the inhabitants by a resurrected Jesus Christ, who came to preach to the natives and to establish his church in the Americas. This translated history came to be called the Book of Mormon, after the ancient author of the history; hence the followers of the religion came to be called Mormons. Within the Church they called themselves "Saints"; all others were called "Gentiles."

Smith's followers considered him to be a prophet, and after the establishment of the church, followed him in the 1830s to settle at Kirtland, near Cleveland, Ohio. There was considerable conflict between church members and the surrounding community, and before long the Mormons were forced to move first to Missouri and then to a settlement they called Nauvoo along the Mississippi shore in Illinois. As the Mormons built their town of

Nauvoo, again there was political and religious conflict as well as rumors of polygamy within the group. And there was occasional vengeance among the Saints themselves. The greatest crisis for the Mormons occurred in 1844, when a mob attacked and murdered Joseph Smith and his brother Hiram while the brothers were being held in jail.

Brigham Young became the successor president of the LDS Church. He believed that the only way for the Mormons to practice their religion in peace and safety was to emigrate from the United States. Not all Mormons followed Young; some, including a brother of Joseph Smith and the first of Smith's many wives, decided to remain behind. This group did not practice polygamy. They formed the still active Reorganized LDS Church (RLDS, now called Community of Christ).

In 1847 Young, like an American Moses, led the first of the wagon treks across the Great Plains to the Great Salt Lake in Utah, which at that time was Mexican territory. Shortly after Utah was ceded to the United States at the conclusion of the 1848 Mexican War, Young applied to Congress to create a vast State of Deseret, which would be under Mormon control. Congress did not comply but instead created the Utah Territory and appointed Young as governor. Between 1847 and the advent of the transcontinental railroad in 1869, an estimated 70,000 converts made the thousand-mile trek across the plains from Nebraska to Utah, burying some 6,000 along the way.

In 1852 the Church officially announced the doctrine of plural marriage, and encouraged it especially among the Church hierarchy. The doctrine was considered a divine revelation of the Prophet, Joseph Smith. Plural marriage "sealed" women to their husbands for eternity, allowing women to achieve a higher level of heavenly life after death. The U.S. Congress reacted by making polygamy illegal, and starting in 1862, passed a number of increasingly punitive acts. These acts were largely ignored or avoided by church members, until the 1882 Edmunds Act and the 1887 Edmunds-Tucker Act escheated all church assets in excess of $50,000, and incarcerated men convicted of polygamy or illegal cohabitation. The Church finally capitulated to the law with the Manifesto of 1890, when Church president Wilford Woodruff had a revelation that resulted in the prohibition of any further plural marriages. Customs and beliefs die slowly, and some illegal plural marriages were still performed after 1890. Polygamous marriages entered into before 1890 were left—unless a man wanted to skip out on his responsibilities—to gradually end in divorce or death.

The Utah Territory was early in permitting women to vote. In 1870 the territorial legislature moved to grant women the franchise, although women were not permitted to hold public office. Congress noted this move with approval, since non-Mormons generally assumed that women in polygamous marriages were little better than slaves, and with the vote they would be able to free themselves. However, Congress was surprised to discover that many of the polygamous wives actively defended the institution of plural marriage. In 1887, the Edmunds-Tucker Act, reinforcing the ban on polygamous marriages, also stripped all Utah women, Mormon or not, of the right to vote.

After the Manifesto of 1890 ending further plural marriages, Congress was willing to consider statehood for Utah. The territory became a state in 1896. Approval of the state constitution incorporated the women's demand for the franchise and the ability to hold elective office; it also incorporated the statements that there would be no further polygamous marriages and no further cohabitation with polygamous wives. The constitution was adopted, and at statehood three women were elected to the first legislature; two to the House and Dr. Martha Hughes Cannon to the Senate, becoming the first woman state senator in the country. The polygamous marriages continued for a time in secret, but finally died out in the principal LDS Church.

The LDS Church is governed by the First Presidency, which consists of the president, who serves for life, and his two counselors. Below this is the Quorum of the Twelve Apostles, who serve for life. The senior member is the president of the Twelve and next in line to become president of the Church. Then there is the Council of the Seventy, whose primary function is to regulate missionary activities. All these groups, along with the Presiding Bishopric, are referred to as the General Authorities.

The Church breaks down its regional control into a number of districts: the "stake" is the administrative unit, a large area of urban and perhaps rural territory, roughly comparable to a diocese. Making up the stake are the wards, which are comparable to parishes, and sometimes a branch, which is a congregation where there are not enough members to form a ward. The ward is presided over by a bishop, with weekly inspirational meetings, Bible study sessions, and social events, which all ward members are expected to attend.

Of the many offshoots of Mormonism, the Reorganized Latter Day Saints (RLDS, now called Community of Christ) located in Independence, Missouri, is the largest after the principal LDS Church of Salt Lake City. This group broke off from the LDS Church over the issue of polygamy, which the then-RLDS Church did not endorse. In Utah, at the time of the Manifesto of 1890 prohibiting further plural marriages, some members refused to give up the practice of polygamy, and later split from the LDS Church. This group, the Fundamentalist LDS Church (FLDS), has split into several polygamist cults located primarily in the western states.

Besides evangelizing throughout the United States, the LDS Church from the beginning has sent its missionaries abroad to bring converts into the fold, first to Great Britain and Europe and now to almost all corners of the world. Today, LDS membership worldwide is estimated by the Church at thirteen million.

CHAPTER 1

Tension between Angus Munn Cannon and his polygamous wife, Martha, must have been great on the night of November 3, 1896, as they waited to learn the results of the election for the first legislature of the new state of Utah. Angus was a Republican, running for state senate from Salt Lake County along with four other "at large" Republicans. Martha, or Mattie as she was called, was a Democrat, running for the same seat as Angus along with four other "at large" Democrats.

The newspapers had great fun with this election: The Democratic *Salt Lake Herald* proclaimed that Mattie, a physician, was the better man of the two; the Republican *Salt Lake Tribune* suggested that Angus Cannon should "go home and break a bouquet over Mrs. Cannon's head to show his superiority."[1] Utah's contest also caught the interest of national newspapers. The *New York Times* commented that "[Mattie] showed her intense independence by declining to follow the political convictions of her husband, who is one of the staunchest Republicans of the state."[2] Their twelve-year-old daughter, Lizzie, reported that her father was "sweating blood" the night before the election. Mattie told Angus, "If I don't win, it's your fault"; however, she later said that she believed he really hoped she would win.[3] Whatever the truth of the feelings on the domestic front, by the next morning it was clear that Elder Angus Munn Cannon, president of the twenty-thousand-member Salt Lake Stake and both brother and nephew to the First Presidency of the Church of Jesus Christ of

Latter-day Saints had suffered an embarrassing loss. Dr. Martha Hughes Cannon had been elected the first woman state senator in the United States.

Martha Maria Hughes was born in 1857 into a Welsh family of recent converts to the Church of Jesus Christ of Latter-day Saints. Her father, Peter Hughes, was a carpenter in the village of Llandudno, Caernarvonshire; her mother, Elizabeth Evans Hughes, was from a prominent family in Birmingham. It is thought that Elizabeth's sister-in-law converted the young couple to the "New Movement" of Mormonism, and the couple was baptized by the Saints of the Welsh Mission of the LDS Church.[4]

Apparently Elizabeth's family was outraged by her conversion. Mormonism was considered by many British to be at best disreputable, more often a scourge upon common decency. In many areas Mormons were actually physically abused. In 1852 a Mormon elder, Orson Pratt, had made the formal announcement that some years earlier, Church founder and prophet Joseph Smith had received a divine revelation concerning the celestial benefits of plural marriage, that is, polygamy, or more precisely polygyny (having multiple wives)—although early there had been a few cases of polyandry (having multiple husbands). Many British who already were baptized into the religion were scandalized and left the Church when the "revelation" became known—such apostasy, in Mormon terms, being an "unpardonable sin."

We do not know if Peter and Elizabeth Hughes were aware of the revelation, or whether they believed, as the Church insisted, that polygamy was divinely ordained. Perhaps they just weren't concerned, because most of the British Mormons, even those who immigrated to Utah, remained monogamous. At any rate the couple caught the "spirit of gathering" and determined to take their two young daughters, Mary Elizabeth, age four, and

Martha Maria, age two, and emigrate from Britain—to Utah, the purported Zion of the New World across the ocean.

Most of the Welsh converts were literate thanks to "circulating schools" that taught people to read so they could read the Bible. The schools tended not to bother with writing, however; hence many of the new converts could read, but they had no idea how to spell even their names. Further, class differences were absolute. The idea of becoming a landowner was almost inconceivable to a Welsh artisan such as Peter Hughes or to the many men who worked in the coal mines. Hence the prospect of owning land across the sea was a major incentive for many of the converts to emigrate.

Elizabeth's parents tried to stop the couple, threatening to use the law to keep them from taking the children out of Britain at the very least. Despite these threats the Hughes managed, perhaps with the help of Elder Thomas Jeremy, head of the Welsh Mission, to get to Liverpool. The family departed Liverpool—departed "Babylon," as the British converts referred to the homeland they perceived as corrupt—arriving a month later in New York.[5]

Peter and Elizabeth did not leave an account of their experiences on board ship. However their voyage was probably typical of those described by other Welsh Saints who had made the trip across the Atlantic. A fellow Welshman, describing his crossing a few years earlier, stated:

Four to six persons were packed into berths of wooden slats measuring six feet square. . . . The passenger would sleep with his feet to the center aisle, where provisions for the voyage, hand luggage and items too fragile for the hold would be stored. Tin utensils and other light items would hang from the side of the berths and from the beams above.[6]

Along with the cramped conditions and the rocking ship came seasickness, especially at the early stages of the voyage, and, according to passengers' journals, the stench of vomit and the lack of sanitation were agonizing.

After the Hughes family finally debarked in New York, their situation became desperate. They were close to penniless, and Peter became seriously ill, unable to work. Elizabeth took in sewing and produced men's neckwear, which she sold. She also gave birth at this time to a third daughter, Annie Lloyd. After two years of struggle in New York, Erastus Snow, an apostle of the new religion, discovered the family's plight. Brother Snow informed them that the Saints in Utah had sent two hundred wagon teams to the frontier in Nebraska to transport to Zion those who didn't have the means. The Hughes family would have a place in one of the church wagons. They were to pack up what goods they still possessed and leave for Nebraska to start the thousand-mile trek across the Great Plains. The Mormon Church had an Emigration Fund from which money was loaned to the faithful to finance the trip to Zion. Brother Snow lent the Hughes sufficient money to join a company of Saints traveling from New York. A wagon in the Joseph Horne Company would be waiting for them at Florence, Nebraska, the settlement on the Missouri River the Mormons referred to as Winter Quarters.

The journey by rail from New York to Nebraska must have been almost unbearable for Elizabeth. Not only did she have a six-year-old, a four-year-old, a baby, and the family's worldly baggage to look after, her husband was extremely ill and would be of little help. The Civil War had broken out just a few months earlier—an event that the Saints knew had been predicted by their prophet, Joseph Smith, many years before. The trains were jammed with troops, many of whom were angry at the sight of the company of Mormons. Mormonism was held in ill repute by many in the United States, principally due to the polygamous marriage practices and the questionable loyalty of Mormons to the United States. Because of the troop transport, there were few railcars available, and frequently the company of Saints had to ride crowded into cattle cars. Several times they had to change trains and wait, sometimes for hours, before progressing farther. Their baggage was dumped from the trains while they waited in Cleveland, Chicago, and Quincy, Illinois. After several hours at Quincy, they boarded the steamer, *Black Hawk*, to Hannibal, Missouri. Here the group was able to buy food supplies, then take another train across Missouri to the Missouri River. The train was traveling through disputed territory; the railroad bridges were being guarded, and earlier some railcars had been fired upon. All along the route the Saints were cursed and abused by drunks and by army enlisted men. Finally, at St. Joseph, they boarded the steamer, *Omaha*, which took them up the Missouri to Florence.[7]

In Florence the Hughes family stayed in an empty house while wagon teams were being organized and cattle and provisions secured. There were some five hundred teams in all, broken down into smaller company units. The Joseph Horne Company, carrying Peter and Elizabeth and their daughters, consisted of fifty-six wagons and a hospital wagon. There were eleven adults assigned to a wagon—thirteen people if there were children— and each adult was allowed to bring only fifty pounds of luggage. There was a total of some six hundred people traveling in Captain Horne's company, along with a few independents with their own teams and provisions.[8]

The pioneer train got underway on the eleventh of July 1861. At an average of fifteen to eighteen miles a day, some sixty days of travel over a thousand miles of rough trail lay ahead before the Saints would reach Zion. Traveling the summer months meant that many kinds of wild food were available along the way. The travelers found wild grapes, currants, cherries, and gooseberries; pigweed they could cook down as greens. Occasionally one of the company would shoot a wild duck or a rabbit or an antelope. Once one of their oxen was killed and divided among them. They slapped mosquitoes, dodged rattlesnakes, and encountered several Indian groups who, although not hostile, demanded provisions. Because this had been anticipated, extra supplies were stocked for such situations. One group of Sioux stopped them, but when told they were Mormons on their way to Utah, they were left alone. Apparently these Sioux previously had had good relations with Mormon travelers.

Traveling over the summer months also meant days of intense heat, occasionally broken by the deluge of a thunderstorm. One day a three-mile-wide prairie fire was visible at a distance, and another day a dust storm descended on the travelers, covering everything, forcing the walkers into the wagons. At night the wagons would form a circle with the cattle inside the round to protect them from being driven off by Indians. Once they were in camp, the men would go in search of water and firewood, although often there was no wood to be found, and dinner was cooked over buffalo chips. In the evenings, if there was time and the travelers were not too exhausted, there might be dances. Sometimes a meeting was held by Brother Erastus Snow or Brother Orson Pratt or Brother Joseph A. Young. Brothers Snow and Pratt had come from Utah to accompany the pioneers and to make sure they crossed safely; Brother Young was the son of Brigham Young and the captain in charge of the entire train of five hundred wagons. Mornings, before leaving camp, the beating of a drum would call the company to prayer.

Peter Hughes became sicker and sicker as the journey progressed. Elizabeth had to walk the entire route so that her husband and children could lie down in the wagon. Her shoes were so worn that they had to be tied round with rags to keep the remnants on. Along the way the pioneers met companies of troops heading east to join up with one side or the other in the war. They also lost several cattle that wandered off. Occasionally the Overland Mail coach would overtake them and disappear into the distance in a cloud of dust, and the wagons passed workers installing the Overland Telegraph as it marched, pole by pole, toward Utah.

The diary of a member of the Horne Company noted that three babies were born during the journey. But there was considerable sickness among the wagon companies. Many of the travelers caught "mountain fever," which was probably typhoid.[9] Thirty-three died along the way. One of the thirty-three was little Annie Lloyd Hughes, scarcely a year old, whose body had to be left along the route. There was no wood for a coffin, and Annie was buried in a shallow grave, covered only by a pile of stones that the family hoped would deter animals from digging.

Annie's death made a great impression on her four-year-old sister, Martha—Mattie, as she had begun to be called. It was the memory of this death, along with others that she was soon to witness, that caused Mattie to decide early in her life that she wanted to do something to stop such suffering in her community. Later, as a young girl, she would become aware that many of the deaths that occurred around her could have been avoided if the patient had had proper treatment. It was this conviction that would send her outside the Mormon community, years later, to study medicine.

The wagons crossed the Continental Divide at South Pass, and, after almost two months of traveling, the train approached Big Mountain. The route was so steep and the wagons so heavy that everyone who was able had to get out and walk. But the reward from the summit was their first view of the Great Salt Lake Valley. For Elizabeth the grueling thousand-mile trek was almost over; for Peter the vision of Zion from the top of Big Mountain would be his last.

The train descended to the pioneers' final camp in Emigrant Canyon. Here the Saints from the city rode to meet the travelers and to take promissory notes from them to cover the cost of their journey. On September 13, 1861, Captain Horne's company rolled into Salt Lake City. Three days later, Peter Hughes was dead.

CHAPTER 2

In September 1861, Elizabeth Hughes was left with two young children in a city unknown to her, with no money and no husband to support the family. However the Saints quickly came to her rescue.[1] As a widow, Elizabeth was entitled to an acre and a quarter of land; the land allocated to her was located at the eastern edge of the city. The mother and her two young children lived in a dugout against a hillside those first months in Zion. Within a year, however, Elizabeth had befriended a Scot carpenter, James Patten Paul, whose wife had died, leaving him with four sons. James and Elizabeth were soon married, and James set about building a house on Elizabeth's land for the combined families. Elizabeth helped him with the construction by making sun-dried adobe bricks. The roof couldn't be finished, however, because they hadn't enough nails to fasten the shingles and lacked the money to buy more. Elizabeth was able to sell some of the clothes she had brought from Wales, a shawl and a broadcloth suit, and bought enough nails with the money for James to finish shingling the roof.

To the six children now in the Paul family, Elizabeth and James together produced five more. There was little money to support such a large family, and the children did what they could to help. Years later, Mattie's daughter Lizzie described how the family lived:

The family picked the native currants that grew along the creeks. They planted fruit pits and seeds they had brought with them across the plains. The children gleaned in the grain fields to feed the pigs. Their lunch was bread spread with sorghum. The girls braided hats of straw and steeped wild sage for a hair tonic. They dressed for parties by "witch lights"—a rag tied around a button that sputtered in a pan of grease. In the early years, a certain sense of humor was needed to keep peace in the household, such as when Elizabeth said to her husband: "Your children and my children are abusing our children."

Before long, however, two of the older boys could leave the family to work on their own, Adam Paul to become a detective and Logan Paul an actor. And Mattie, at age fourteen, became a schoolteacher. That job lasted only a year, however, because the boys in her classroom were bigger than she was. Some of them were not much interested in learning anything, and she couldn't control them. At the end of the school term, she gladly turned the class over to her seventeen-year-old sister, Mary.

Fortunately for Mattie, she was asked by the Church president, Brigham Young, if she would like to learn typesetting. Anything seemed better than teaching school, and she and two other girls became apprenticed to Brother Hyrum Perry, the printer who managed the print shop for the *Deseret News*, the newspaper of the LDS Church. The editor of the *News* was George Q. Cannon, an apostle in the Church; the business manager was George's brother, Angus, a man who would later play a major role in Mattie's life. Day after day Mattie's job was to pick up the tiny leaden slugs, one by one, and notch them together in position. She became so adept at this that in addition to setting type for the *News*, she was able to set type for the Church's publications in Scandinavian languages, although she had no idea what the words meant. By learning to set foreign-language type, she was able to earn extra money.

Boring as this work must have been for an intelligent girl, Mattie found that typesetting had certain rewards. She was able to read the articles for the newspaper, and later, when she set type for the *Woman's Exponent*, the Mormon women's magazine, she became aware of articles relating to events both national and international, particularly as they applied to women.

It was about this time that Mattie began to consider the possibility of studying medicine. Working on the magazine opened her eyes to opportunities for women that she otherwise might not have been aware of. Not only did the magazine broaden her interests, as a result of setting type for it, she also met several outstanding women who were powerful in the LDS Church, especially Emmeline Wells, the editor of the *Exponent*. Mattie also caught the attention of the woman who was considered the "Matriarch of Mormonism," Eliza Snow. Eliza was the most influential woman in Salt Lake. She had been married to Joseph Smith, the Prophet, and after Smith's murder, she became a plural wife of Brigham Young. She was quite elderly when Mattie met her, but Eliza recognized Mattie's intelligence and became a mentor to the girl.

Mattie had read in the *Exponent* that in 1870 the University of Michigan had opened its medical school to women, and she determined that someday she would study there. In order to be eligible to enter, however, she would have to have a university degree. She began to spend some of her carefully hoarded savings on medical books. Both Emmeline Wells and Eliza Snow encouraged her, and in 1876 Mattie enrolled at Deseret University (now the University of Utah). She kept the typesetting job during the day and took classes at the university at night.

Up until the early 1870s, the medical situation in Mormon Utah, as generally in the West, was at best primitive. In addition to their work with expectant mothers, midwives provided much of the general medical assistance, everything from pulling teeth to minor surgery. Unlike some societies, where the accomplishments of midwives were often viewed with suspicion and their power to heal ascribed to witchcraft, LDS Church authorities called women to midwifery and blessed them to carry out their work. In the Mormon Church, a "call" is a command, and this call gave the midwife status. Claire Noall, in her article on Mormon midwives, notes that at the time she was writing some superstitions still obtained.[2] She recounts a legend that a rusty axe placed in bed with the mother keeps down afterpains, and another in which a woman, bitten on her neck and arms by mice, worried that her unborn child would be similarly marked. If a woman wanted a daughter, she lay on one side after coitus, and if a son, she lay on the other. That superstitions regarding the mysteries of birth were not so widespread among the nineteenth-century Saints as among other groups is probably due to the strength of their religious beliefs. The legends and myths that were held to by some of the women were not the beliefs of the midwife herself. Indeed, many of the Mormon midwives were experienced and well skilled, some of them successfully delivering hundreds of babies under trying frontier conditions. This is not to say that Mormons did not believe in miracles. Miracles were considered a manifestation of God's grace, rather than the influence of a rusty axe or a mouse attack. Because the Saints believed untimely death to be God's will, if the midwife failed to save a child or prevent an infection or a death, she was not held responsible.

The few doctors practicing among the Saints were steeped in the theories of Samuel Thomson, an herbalist with no formal medical training, who developed a practice of medicine based on the idea that health and disease are a manifestation of hot and cold energies. The regulation of heat and cold in the body was to be achieved by use of a variety of natural herbs, the most important of which were lobelia and capsicum (red pepper). A few of the doctors had had some schooling, and one had actually attended Samuel Thomson's fourteen-week course in Boston. Most, however, simply used Thomson's *New Guide to Health*, which could be purchased, along with a certificate to practice, for $20.[3]

But even Thomsonism was an improvement over some of the ideas about remedies that were common to frontier folklore: Mouth odor was eliminated by daily rinsing of the mouth with urine; mashed snails and earthworms in water were good for treating diphtheria; an onion in your pocket prevented small-pox; mashed cabbage cured ulcers and breast cancer; broth of an owl cured whooping cough; two tablespoons of India ink cured tapeworm. To relieve toothache, the gums should be scratched with an iron nail until they bleed, and then the nail must be pounded into a wooden beam. (Toothache must have been com-mon on the frontier, for although toothbrushes began to appear in stores by the late 1850s, not everyone knew to use them. Most people were toothless by the time they reached fifty.[4])

As a child in New York State in the 1820s, the Prophet, Joseph Smith, had had bad experiences with "regular doctors." He lost a brother to what he believed was the ignorance of the doctor. The doctor had prescribed calomel, which was the typical treat-ment for the boy's symptoms—the treatment for just about any-thing at the time. The boy died because his intestines became gangrenous from being plugged with the calomel. Smith, him-self, almost lost an infected leg to a doctor who could think of nothing better to do than to cut it off. Smith's mother refused to have her son's leg amputated and was convinced she had saved the leg through her prayers.

The regular—or orthodox—medical profession, such as it was at that time, believed that most infections could be cured by bleeding the patient, and for most everything else, calomel and laudanum were the drugs of choice. Priddy Meeks, a self-taught

Thomsonian, writes in his journal that he considered the drugs of the orthodox doctors "as poisonous a catalog of articles as might be needed to kill a man." Priddy's remedy for just about any affliction was lobelia.[5]

Joseph Smith warned his people to avoid the "poisonous medicines." Such "poisons" were tools of the devil, and included calomel, laudanum, iodine, and various purges and emetics. And in his "Word of Wisdom" in the *Doctrine and Covenants*, one of several of the books he wrote to guide his people, he cautions against tobacco, alcohol, tea, coffee, and meat, except this last might be permitted in winter. The sick must rely on natural herbs for medicine, as well as religious ministrations—prayer, anointing with oil, and the laying on of hands. If the herbs and ministrations were not successful, then God had made His decision.

During these years diphtheria, typhoid, and infantile diarrhea caused the greatest number of childhood deaths.[6] Ignorance of the need for sanitation caused countless women to die in childbirth from puerperal fever. Such infectious diseases as smallpox, scarlet fever, typhoid, diphtheria, yellow fever, cholera, and tuberculosis were rampant throughout the country, tuberculosis being the greatest cause of death in adults both in the United States and Europe. Clearly Thomsonian herbs, though they may have had positive effects in certain cases, were not adequate to head off the effects of these epidemics. Yet as late as the 1860s, Brigham Young stated, "Doctors and their medicines I regard as deadly bane to any community."[7]

The arrival of the intercontinental railroad in 1869 threatened the hegemony of the LDS Church. The railroad would make immigration of Mormon converts easier than trekking across the plains, but it would also bring additional "Gentiles" to settle in the territory. President Young worried the influx of Gentiles would inevitably bring political, social, and economic pressures to bear on the Saints. He urged the people to become proficient in all fields of study so they could remain independent of Gentile influence.

Young's efforts to build a theocracy in the Utah Territory necessitated a communitarian approach to social organization. Everyone had to work to advance the society. The men worked to physically build Zion and to proselytize abroad for new converts. The women not only had to help with the farms and participate in early communal economic ventures such as raising silkworms, making articles out of straw, spinning and weaving cloth, and working in the cooperative stores, but it also was expected of them to provide the baby Saints that would satisfy the Old Testament stricture to "multiply and subdue the earth." Because of the need for an ever-increasing population to expand Mormon control in the territory, as well as the emphasis on becoming educated in the professions as a hedge against Gentile influence, many women enjoyed a position of influence, both religious and political, at this point in the development of the society. It was a position that in later years would not hold.

By the early 1870s, President Young finally realized that the "old ways" advocated by the Prophet in his "Word of Wisdom" were no longer adequate to protect the Saints from the influence of "Gentile medicine" coming into Utah, nor from the epidemics that periodically attacked the community. The practice of medicine by this time had progressed somewhat beyond the "poison" doctors of the past. Young reversed himself in his belief in purely herbal and theological remedies, and in 1872 sent his nephew Seymour Bicknell Young to the New York College of Physicians and Surgeons.[8] Soon the president was sending other men to study at medical schools in the East.

Very likely Young's change of heart regarding orthodox medicine was the result of his friendship with Dr. Washington Anderson. Although not a Mormon, Dr. Anderson was respectful of Mormon orderliness under President Young's control. He became a confidant of the president and was involved in community affairs. In the 1870s Dr. Anderson was elected head of the first medical society in Utah and served for several years on the Board of Examiners. The drugs that the Thomsonians were so against—calomel, the bromides, potassium iodide, ferric chloride, and the various opiates—were the mainstays of Dr. Anderson's practice.[9] Young's wife, Eliza Snow, was adamant that a scientific approach to medicine was needed in the greater Mormon community, and that women should prepare themselves for such work, at least in so far as the needs of women patients were concerned. Undoubtedly through Eliza's influence, in 1873 President Young singled out women as well as men for medical education, stating, "The time has come for women to come forth as doctors in these valleys of the mountains."[10]

Young was concerned that if his people turned to non-Mormon (i.e., "Gentile") doctors and other professionals, his control over the settlements would diminish. Eliza was concerned about the propriety of allowing male doctors to treat female patients, and she was especially concerned to keep men out of the delivery room. She said at a meeting in 1873 that "we want sister physicians who can officiate in any capacity that the gentlemen are called upon to officiate, and unless they educate themselves, the gentlemen that are flocking in our midst will do it."[11] One historian notes that at the time it was thought "a woman who employed a male doctor to wait upon her in illness was possessed of an adulterous spirit."[12] For all the frontier roughness, this was indeed, even in far off Utah, the Victorian era.

This concern with the need for educated woman physicians in the Mormon community spurred Mattie's ambition. She had not forgotten her grief at the death of little Annie Lloyd and at the death of her father, for both of whom no professional treatment could have been available. Additionally she was surrounded with the deadly diseases that prevailed in the West.

She had watched many a child die of diphtheria, or become deaf from scarlet fever, or become scarred for life from the plague of smallpox. From her reading she knew that a vaccine against smallpox was available, and had been for some years, although the immunization was not lasting and sometimes had serious side effects. Robert Koch and Louis Pasteur were developing the "germ theory," which would lead to an understanding of bacteria as a cause of disease. Deadly puerperal fever was the result of bacteria from the unclean hands that assisted the birthing process, and while many experienced midwives and doctors were aware of this and took precautions to make sure their ministrations were sanitary, many still did not, with tragic consequences. Because of the lack of adequate sanitation facilities, Salt Lake City was rife with typhoid, and men working in the mines were contracting silicosis, which often turned into pulmonary tuberculosis. Mattie felt called to educate the Saints to the importance of public health. In her dream of becoming a doctor, Mattie had the support of Eliza Snow and Emmeline Wells. She also had the support of her stepfather James Paul, who believed in her, encouraged her, and promised to do what he could to help her. Mattie's problem was finding the money to get to Michigan and to stay there for the two years it would take her to get her MD degree.

After paying her board at her parents' house, she had saved as much as possible in the years that she studied in the university while working as a typesetter. Rather than take the mule-drawn streetcar, which would be an added expense, she walked as much as six miles to get to work, then to the university, then back home. The oiled shoes that women wore in the winter were inadequate to keep her feet dry during such long walks, and Mattie ordered a pair of men's boots to be made for her. She wore the boots through the snow and mud with her skirts hiked up to her knees and carried her more ladylike shoes in a bag to wear when she arrived at her destination. She was so busy working and studying that caring for her long hair seemed too much bother. She cut it short—a shocking transgression, along with the boots, of the Victorian image of female beauty and propriety.

In 1878 Mattie graduated from Deseret University with a degree in chemistry. The University of Michigan found the Deseret degree adequate for her to qualify for entry to the medical school, and Mattie prepared for her departure to Ann Arbor. Earlier, she had wavered for a moment in her resolve and let her emotions take over: She had come close to marrying someone with whom she had let herself become deeply involved. Certainly many in the society expected that she would marry; she was already twenty-one years old, older than many of the marriageable girls. But her ambition won out, and she broke the promise of her engagement.

Her carpenter stepfather made her a trunk to take her clothes and books to Michigan and promised to send her what he could afford—ten dollars every month as a loan. Eliza Snow knitted her a purse and tucked a twenty-dollar gold piece in it. Mattie requested permission to use the hall of the Tenth Ward for a fund-raising benefit to help pay for her trip. She had been the secretary of the Tenth Ward Retrenchment Society—a young women's organization—and had taught in the ward Sunday school. The ward often held benefits for young men setting off as missionaries, and the bishop decided that Sister Martha Hughes Paul's departure to medical school certainly justified a send-off party. Brigham Young had earlier stated that he was willing to "set her apart"—a Mormon phase meaning to be chosen for a special mission—to pursue her studies in Michigan, but he did not live long enough to do that. George Q. Cannon, one of the Church apostles and the editor of the *Deseret News* for whom Mattie had worked, set her apart, blessed her, and sent her on her way.

CHAPTER 3

Mattie was not the first woman in Mormon Utah to receive a medical education. In the 1850s three women doctors had come to Utah—Netta Cardon, Janet Hardie, and Vigdis Holt. All three had studied medicine and practiced in Europe, although it is not known if they had actually earned medical degrees. At that time a woman would have to go to Europe to study because they weren't welcome in the regular medical schools in the United States. However, even in Europe the state of medical knowledge was not much advanced. Bloodletting was still a standard practice, and until 1865, when the British physician Joseph Lister introduced antisepsis into surgery, doctors did not understand how to prevent infection. Surgeons might operate wearing their street clothes, not even washing their hands. Hence on the frontier, until knowledge of the use of carbolic acid as a disinfectant became widespread, surgeries often led to serious or fatal infections.[1]

During the late 1870s another woman doctor, Ellen Ferguson, arrived in Utah with her physician husband. Apparently Ellen did not actually have a medical degree, but she had studied medicine in England and had learned from her husband sufficiently to practice in Europe and the United States. This seemed in her mind to justify advertising for her services as *Dr.* Ellen Ferguson. Converted to Mormonism, Ellen started a practice in Utah and in 1878 organized classes for women in obstetrics and the diseases of women and children. Having been given an extensive private education by her father, a Cambridge professor, she also taught classes in French, Latin, German, drawing, elocution, drama, and music. In addition to these varied talents, she was an avid feminist, and she became the first woman deputy sheriff in the United States.[2]

Mattie was one of three women in the 1870s called to study medicine by the Church. The first was Romania Bunnell Pratt, a thirty-four-year-old mother of five, who sold her home and piano in 1874, left the children with her mother, and went to study in New York. She became the first woman admitted to Bellevue College, a part of Bellevue Hospital, and excelled in dissection, which was a challenge for a woman student, not the least because of the cost of the cadaver—$40 split among four students. When Romania couldn't afford to continue her studies a second year, she returned home, but Brigham Young urged the Relief Society—the Mormon women's society that was set up to aid the poor—to raise the money to allow her to continue. With the Relief Society's help, Romania returned East, this time to the Woman's Medical College of Pennsylvania in Philadelphia. Established in 1850, the college was the second orthodox medical school for women in the United States.[3] Romania earned her MD in 1877, specializing in ear and eye surgery.

In 1875 Ellis Shipp, a plural wife of Milford Shipp, left her children with her sister-wife Margaret and joined Romania at the Woman's College in Philadelphia. At the end of the second year, she gave birth to her fourth child but continued her studies while a landlady took care of the baby. Along with money sent by her sister-wife, Ellis financed her schooling while working as a dressmaker, completing her MD in 1878. She returned to Salt Lake to establish her practice and begin teaching classes in obstetrics and nursing. Five years later, her sister-wife Margaret got her MD, also from the Woman's Medical College. Not to be outdone by his wives, Milford got his MD from Philadelphia's

Jefferson Medical College. Ellis, Margaret, and Milford published the first medical journal in Utah, the *Salt Lake Sanitarian.* Although the journal survived only three years, it issued warnings to the community about polluted water and the dangers of the lack of sanitation facilities. It reported on the danger to children from diarrhea caused by impure milk, and presented articles on the theories of Koch and Pasteur and other medical research. It also advised that male baldness was due to lack of sunlight on the head, and that men should wash their heads weekly and always wear ventilated hats.

As often happens when one member of a marriage is off studying for some years, the marriage, even a polygamous marriage, cannot survive the separation. Romania's marriage to Parley Pratt Jr. and Margaret's marriage to Milford Shipp ended in divorce not long after the two women returned to Salt Lake City.

Mattie Hughes Paul—she chose to use her stepfather's name in this period of her life—was the third woman that Brigham Young called to study medicine. He had taken an interest in her while she was still a student at Deseret University. She did not leave much of a record of her studies at the University of Michigan's School of Medicine. There is only a copy of one of her class notebooks in the LDS Church archives in which she lists the effects, in her distinctive, scribbled handwriting, of various medicines. She does not mention in any extant letters male harassment in medical school, although it is very likely she experienced it. In the nineteenth century women were not welcome in most regular medical schools, even if officially allowed entrance. When the University of Michigan decided in 1870 to admit women—an experiment considered of "doubtful utility" by some of the faculty—it was agreed that men and women could not be taught in the same classroom. Mattie and her fellow female colleagues had to sit in a separate room where the male students couldn't see them.[4]

Mattie as a young woman, ca. 1880

Along with a general conviction of the inferiority of women prevalent in American society and protests and occasional riots by male students at medical schools where women were admitted, many professors refused to discuss anatomy in the presence of the delicate sex. There was a gynecological theory current that intellectual activity was injurious to the female reproductive organs. Some of this was the belief that women were just too frail and delicate to withstand the assaults on their modesty, inevitable in the study of anatomy. However, some of it was undoubtedly a conspiracy of the male medical establishment to maintain a monopoly on the doctor business. Not only did many men fear competition with women, but also many male doctors had a lucrative business administering to the bored, hypochondriac wives of wealthy husbands.[5]

Women like Mattie who braved male-dominated medical schools in the 1870s were a tough lot. They had to ignore the Victorian cult of female frailty that was the vogue among the middle and upper classes; many had to fight the stigma of impropriety and sometimes outright hostility from their own families and social communities. Amanda Sanford, who graduated from the University of Michigan a few years before Mattie, received her MD degree with honors, along with being "hooted and showered with abusive notes."[6] Mattie was perhaps more fortunate than most women in that she had the support of a tight-knit religious community back home that was counting on her success. The education of Mattie and her women colleagues was far superior to the standard medical education up until the 1880s. Until then all a man needed to do was to spend a year learning in a doctor's office, and then take two winter courses of four months each in a medical school.

Mattie's savings and the money received from her stepfather were not enough to support her during the two years it took for her to get her MD degree. During her first year she worked as a maid in a student dormitory, washing dishes and making beds. Circumstances were better her second year when she got a job as the secretary to a fellow student, Bethenia Owens-Adair. Owens-Adair was seventeen years older than Mattie, and she had already studied at the Philadelphia's Eclectic School of Medicine in 1870. Owens-Adair received her MD degree the same year as Mattie and went on to become the first woman doctor in Oregon, and, as Mattie would later become, an avid suffragist.

Mattie took all the prescribed courses needed to graduate, studied extra courses at night in pharmacology, and did additional work in electro-therapeutics and bacteriology. This last must have been a new course in the medical curriculum, since Koch and Pasteur's "germ theory"—the theory that certain diseases and infections are caused by the spread of bacteria in the environment—was only beginning to be understood. She received her degree, *Doctoris in Arte Medica*, on her twenty-third birthday in the summer of 1880.

Mattie spent the next year in Algonac, a small Michigan town on the Canadian border, where she had her chance to practice medicine for the first time. Her first case involved a riverboat captain's wife who was mentally ill. Mattie discovered the cause of the malady and was able to heal the woman of her insanity. Another case was a surgery, a case of vesico-vaginal fistula—an abnormal connection between the urinary tract and the vagina. The local newspaper reported that one doctor had refused to assist Mattie in the surgery because he would not "play second-fiddle to a woman," but two other male doctors had agreed to be her assistants—apparently without experiencing any loss of dignity. The operation was a success, and the newspaper went on to praise Dr. Paul as a "genial and accomplished woman, who not only graduated from the Medical Department of Michigan University with a reputation for superior scholarship, but is possessed of . . . courage and self-reliance."[7]

In the fall of 1881, Mattie left Algonac to continue her studies in Philadelphia. Margaret Shipp was still at the Woman's Medical College there, but instead of joining Margaret, Mattie entered the Auxiliary Medical Department of the University of Pennsylvania for postgraduate training. The department was founded in 1865, but it did not admit women until three years before Mattie entered. This graduate program focused on collateral branches of medical science, and the courses included a variety of subjects such as medical jurisprudence and toxicology, which included forensic medicine, and geology, which discussed the geographic range of diseases. The curriculum also included botany, mineralogy, hygiene, comparative anatomy, and zoology. On successful completion of the courses and acceptance of a thesis, the student would receive a Bachelor of Science degree.

Mattie's thesis, still available in the library at the University of Pennsylvania, was a study of "mountain fever." Mountain fever was a serious problem in the Rocky Mountains. Brigham Young had been stricken with it on his initial crossing of the prairies and was extremely ill and weak when he finally arrived in the Great Salt Lake Basin in 1847. At the time mountain fever was thought to be typhoid. Mattie's study of the disease determined that

> *Mountain Fever is a malarial fever, differing from the malarial fever of the swamps only in the mode of entrance of the poison into the system. In the latter by pulmonary absorption of volatile emanations; in the former (Mountain Fever) by admission into the stomach in watery solution.*

Mattie determined that quinine would cure mountain fever within a few days, whereas it had no affect on typhoid.[8]

Mattie received her BS degree at the 1882 graduation ceremony of the Auxiliary Medical Department. The graduation program shows that law and medical degrees were given to several male students, but Martha P. Hughes, MD, was the only woman to receive the BS degree.

Although Mattie's plan was to open a practice when she returned to Utah, she had not lost sight of her goal to teach her community the importance of public health. To this end she enrolled in the National School of Elocution and Oratory, a leading institute of public speaking, concurrently with her science studies at the university. Apparently she had quite a flair for dramatics, since her instructors thought she should concentrate on becoming an actress.[9] She received a Bachelor of Oratory in June of 1882.

The intensity of her work in Philadelphia finally took its toll on her health, and late in 1882, Mattie returned to her parents' home in Salt Lake City with meningitis—brain fever, as it was then called—the inflammation of the membranes that surround and protect the central nervous system.

As attractive and intelligent a young woman as Mattie would be bound to leave some broken hearts in her wake as she pursued her ambitions. In addition to the young man she broke with after she left Utah for Michigan, a couple more along the way lost hope of her hand. One of these, a beau from Philadelphia, went so far as to convert to Mormonism and follow her back to Salt Lake. Her stepfather welcomed the young man to live with the family. This must have been difficult for Mattie, who was recovering from her illness, as well as for the hopeful suitor, who was getting nowhere in his courtship. He finally gave up and left, and Mattie was soon well enough to start her practice. In a letter to a Philadelphia school chum, Barbara Replogle, Mattie describes her illness: Her doctor has forbidden "all manner of brain work, even reading and writing," but she has ignored him. She is very happy: "How I love my dear old Rocky Mountains . . . and my father's little cottage under the hill." She mentions in this letter a theme that will recur throughout her correspondence with Barbara over the years: the importance of a woman's intellectual ambition. She praises Barbara for her choice of lifework—elocution and literature. "Nowhere outside the maternal circle does woman shine in her full glory as on the platform."[10]

James Paul built a wing onto his house on Ninth East as an office for his stepdaughter. Mattie began receiving patients in her new quarters and purchased a horse and buggy for house calls. Apparently she had many patients, for she mentions in the same letter to Replogle that her practice is "remunerative and my old ambition is returning." Hence she was able to help out her family and pay back her debts. Educated women doctors were still rare in Utah, and they did a good business—sometimes too good a business in the opinion of certain male doctors, who were said to grumble of "petticoat domination."

The Deseret Hospital was established by a group of activist women, under the leadership of Eliza Snow, while Mattie was still in Philadelphia. The group had met with Church President John Taylor to discuss a Latter-day Saints hospital in Salt Lake City. The women argued that a hospital was needed that would be specifically oriented to the ministrations of the priesthood. The Saints should be able to introduce their own religious healing practices as an important adjunct to the new ideas and treatments that the recent medical students were bringing back from the eastern colleges and universities. Further, a place was needed where midwives could train. The women doctors were holding classes for students from all over Utah who wished to be nurses and midwives, but there was no place to give them the necessary clinical demonstrations and practice. The group did not see their proposal as merely a lying-in hospital; they anticipated a general hospital for all members of the community, but one at which their own elders could "walk freely in and perform the ceremonies of the Church without having the eyes of the curious upon them."[11]

The women raised funds from the Relief Society and the Young Ladies Mutual Improvement Association and received some monies from general Church funds. They devised a plan to meet the cost of operational expenses: A premium payment of a dollar a year would be solicited from every member of every ward and stake in Utah Mormondom. If a family was too poor to pay, produce or work could be accepted. In addition to the individual annual dollars, every Relief Society and other Church organizations would be required to contribute a dollar a month to establish ward credit accounts. Those who were capable of paying for their care would be required to do so; those who could not would be covered by the communal funds.

The Deseret Hospital would be the third hospital in Utah. Ten years earlier, St. Mark's Hospital had been established by Episcopalians in Salt Lake City in response to the 1869 arrival of the transcontinental railroad. The advent of the railroad suddenly made mining an economic enterprise in the Wasatch and other Utah locations. Although extensive lead deposits, as well as silver and gold, had been discovered before 1869, there was no practical way of shipping the material out of the territory. But with the coming of the train, mines could be developed and smelters built. Consequently a hospital was also needed to take care of the inevitable mining accidents, and what would subsequently become a major health problem: lead poisoning. The lead deposits were in the form of carbonates, and in many places they were so soft they could be easily shattered by a pick. The miners were being poisoned by inhaling the lead dust.

The Deseret women perhaps got their idea for financing their hospital services from the mining companies. The companies generously supported St. Mark's, and each company miner paid a dollar a month into a fund that entitled him to a bed and care whenever he should need it. Apparently some of the miners wanted the Catholic Church to sponsor a hospital as well, and Holy Cross Hospital opened its doors in a renovated barn that almost immediately became inadequate—the nurses had to sleep on the floor. In 1882 Holy Cross Hospital purchased a large ten-acre tract at the edge of the city, and the Deseret women were able to take over the vacated Catholic barn with a twelve-bed hospital. Two years later they were able to move to a much larger building vacated by the University of Deseret. Calling again on the Relief Society, the Young Ladies Mutual Improvement Association, and general Church funds, the Saints raised money to travel to New York to buy the latest medical equipment for their new project. The resident physician—the only paid position—was Dr. Ellen Ferguson, and the visiting physicians were Brigham Young's early friend, Dr. Washington Anderson; Brigham's nephew, Dr. Seymour Young; eye and ear specialist Romania Pratt; and Dr. Ellis Shipp.

Mattie was still developing her private practice when she received the call from the Church authorities to be the resident physician for the Deseret Hospital. She would be replacing Dr. Ferguson, who was leaving to continue her private practice. For Mattie this meant giving up her own practice, but for a devout Mormon as she was, such a call would be obeyed without question. When Mattie took over the resident physician position, the hospital was charging $3 per day for care, a charge that soon rose to $6—a dollar in the 1880s would be worth about $21 today.

St. Mark's Hospital was, with a few exceptions, exclusively for the mining industry, and the Saints were uncomfortable administering their Mormon rituals in the Catholic hospital. At the Deseret Hospital the priesthood could carry out their religious ministrations for the patients and could hold their group prayer sessions. The hospital enjoyed a well-trained medical staff, and although technically a full-care hospital, the focus was on obstetrical cases. Mattie had the opportunity to establish training classes for nurses, where she lectured on obstetrics.

The hospital was headed by a board of directors, and one of the directors was Angus Munn Cannon. Cannon was president of the huge Salt Lake Stake, and brother to Apostle George Q. Cannon, a member of the Twelve, the highest Church authority under the First Presidency.[12] There is a story that one day Mattie rather peremptorily told Elder Angus Munn Cannon to leave the room so that she could get on with her work.[13] The nurse assistants were appalled that a woman would have the audacity to speak in such a manner to a member of the Church hierarchy. Apparently such feistiness appealed to Elder Cannon. Within the year Mattie secretly became his fourth polygamous wife.

CHAPTER 4

From the earliest days of the Church of Jesus Christ of Latter-day Saints, there was animosity between Church members and non-Mormons from the surrounding communities. Not that the Saints were the innocent victims of this animosity. Both Mormons and non-Mormons participated in retaliatory violence, resulting, in 1838, in an Extermination Order on the heads of the Mormons, issued by the governor of Missouri.[1] There was conflict within the saintly group as well; for example, when the Mormon police captain in Nauvoo stated that the appropriate response to an apostate was to "cut him off—behind the ears—according to the law of God in such cases."[2]

In part the Saints' troubles were caused by an attitude of communal exclusivity encouraged by the Church authorities. In his *History of Utah*, the nineteenth-century historian Hubert Howe Bancroft noted the "impudence" and "arrogance" of the Mormons, and that the real difficulty being the "impossibility of others living with them as members of one community."[3] Such exclusiveness, however, is the defensive reaction of a people abused for their beliefs and hounded from one state to another until they are finally forced to make their biblical Exodus to the uncharted deserts of the West.

But what attacked the American sense of "common decency" and the Victorian notion of "true womanhood" and led to diatribes from church pulpits, the press, and the government was the practice by certain members of the Mormon hierarchy, including their self-styled prophet president, of polygamy. The famous antislavery activist and author Harriet Beecher Stowe deemed polygamy "a slavery which debases and degrades womanhood, motherhood, and family."[4] Rumors of polygamy among the Mormons had been circulating since the 1830s, although for the first years, Church leaders denied the practice, attempting to deceive their own members as well as the public at large. The revelation of "celestial marriage" wasn't officially announced as Church doctrine until 1852, when the initial settlers and their leaders were safe in their territorial redoubt.

Despite the general uproar over the practice, polygamy wasn't illegal in the federal territories until the first federal anti-bigamy act, the Morrill Act, was passed in 1862. Nevertheless, at the state level the practice was illegal in Illinois at the time the Mormons were living in Nauvoo. Washington, however, was much too busy fighting a war to be overly concerned about the conjugal habits of a group of settlers isolated in the Wild West. The Morrill Act not only criminalized polygamy, it also annulled the articles of incorporation of the LDS Church and restricted Church ownership of property to an asset value of less that $50,000. Any Church property valued in excess of that amount was subject to government confiscation. The act wasn't enforced, and the Saints ignored it, continuing to advocate plural marriage, especially among the Church authorities and those seeking to gain acceptance into the hierarchy. Busy with a war on his hands, Abraham Lincoln is reported to have said: "Tell Brigham Young that if he will leave me alone, I'll leave him alone."[5]

For the Saints the call to plural marriage may have been divinely ordained, but apparently it was never fully accepted, or at least never practiced by all Church members. It is estimated that during the nineteenth century, only a quarter to a third of Mormon marriages were polygamous, and of those most involved only two wives. Toward the end of the century, perhaps only

10 percent of the marriages were polygamous. It was the leaders who had the conjugal harems: Brigham Young was purported to have had twenty-seven wives and fifty-six children. No one was quite sure of the number sealed to the Prophet Joseph Smith— approximately thirty-three wives is an estimate, twelve of whom were concurrently married to another man.[6] In many ways Mormon polygamy followed the pattern of other polygamous societies. Robert Wright, in his study, *The Moral Animal*, compares polygynous and monogamous societies, and notes that

> *even where it is "common," multiple wives are generally reserved for a relatively few men who can afford them or qualify for them via formal rank. For eons and eons, most marriages have been monogamous, even though most societies haven't been.*[7]

There was another aspect of the Utah colony that caused considerable concern in Washington: the concern over the Mormon position toward the Civil War. The Saints didn't join either side in the war, although they believed slavery to be a divine institution since it had biblical authority. In 1852 Brigham Young had instructed the territorial legislature to legalize slavery because it was important that the Saints believe in it. There were few slaves in Utah, although some were bought and sold before 1862, when U.S. law abolished slavery in the territories.

Although most of the Church leaders were originally from the North and might be expected to sympathize with the Union, they had not forgotten their persecutions in Ohio, Illinois, and Missouri. They had a passionate concern for the Southerners' issue of states' rights and believed that if Utah could become a state, such rights would allow them to maintain their precious principle of polygamy. Further, treasonous statements from Mormon pulpits worried many in Washington. Joseph Smith had predicted the Civil War in a revelation in 1832, and that it would begin, as indeed it did, in South Carolina, and that the Southerners would call on Great Britain for help, which indeed they did. Many of the leaders saw the effectuation of the Prophet's revelation as a sign that the Millennium was at hand. The two sides would destroy each other, and the Kingdom of God, administered by the Latter-day Saints, would soon rule over the ruins of the country. Greatly concerned, the Gentile governor of Utah reported to Secretary of State William Seward the content of a speech Brigham Young had given:

> *Nothing can save the Government of the United States. It could have been saved if the people had accepted Joseph Smith Junior for their President when he offered himself. But the people rejected him, as the Jews rejected the Savior when he was upon the earth; and as they were destroyed for their wickedness, so will the people of the American Government be . . . Perhaps some may say this is treason—well I admit if this is treason, I am treasonous. My people are all treasoners if this is treason.*[8]

Despite his concern for states' rights, Brigham Young was smart enough not to support the South, and toward the war's end, after it had become clear which side would prevail, the Saints came around to supporting the North.

After the war, and especially after the arrival of the transcontinental railroad into Utah, the government no longer ignored the violation of its laws by the Mormons. Prodded by non-Mormons determined to break the Saints' monopoly on commerce, manufacturing, and agriculture in the territory, as well as by the antipolygamy agitation of the American public, Congress was moved to do something about "the Mormon question." Still, prosecutions cost money, and when U.S. Attorney George Caesar Bates wrote the Justice Department in 1871, complaining that there were no funds to try Brigham Young for polygamy, his request for help was ignored. In 1873, when Judge E. B. McKean ousted the Mormon-appointed territorial marshal, he found himself in turn ousted from his courtroom by the Mormon landlords of the building. For the next eighteen months, the Third District Court met in a hayloft over a livery stable. Courtrooms had to be rented, and for a time in the 1880s, the court met in rooms below a brothel. Washington finally sent enough money for the court to rent the upper floor as well, thus removing "the objectionable parties." After leaving office, U.S. Attorney Bates as well as several other U.S. attorneys became counsel for the LDS Church. Apparently the Church paid better than the government.[9]

In 1874 Congress passed the Poland Act. Prior to this time, the Church controlled the probate courts, and civil and criminal cases were held in these courts under the jurisdiction of Mormon judges. Under such conditions it was not likely that an antipolygamy statute would be enforced. The Poland Act transferred all civil and criminal cases to the jurisdiction of federal district courts under the territorial district attorneys, leaving the Mormon-controlled probate courts to settle only matters of inheritance, guardianship, or divorce.

The Church considered the bonding in marriage and the breaking of that bond through divorce strictly a religious matter. Records of these unions and dissolutions were kept only by the local stakes or wards. There was no civil registration of marriages or divorces in the territory until 1887, and this allowed polygamists to hide from the law. The federal courts would not acknowledge that a plural wife's marriage was legal in the first place and hence could not grant a divorce. A divorce in the probate court was quite easy for the Saints, demonstrating that women were not held captive as polygamous sex slaves, contrary to what the rest of America may have thought. If a man or a woman were unhappy in a marriage, or if a woman in a polygamous marriage could not get along with the other wives, President Young would grant a divorce; however, the husband had to pay Young a fee of ten dollars.[10] Young did not countenance unhappiness and disharmony within the community. For a time the easy attitude of the Saints toward divorce turned the courts of Mormon Utah into a divorce mill for Gentiles.[11] Hence, ironically, Mormon marital practices conflicted with the values of the greater society in two opposing ways: the practice of polygamy and the easy access to divorce.

Since bigamy was illegal under the Morrill Act and there were no civil marriage records, plural wives and their children had no legal claim to an inheritance unless the husband or father provided for them in his will, or the legitimate first wife voluntarily agreed to share among her sister-wives. This situation was only slightly improved by the passage of the Edmunds Act in 1882, which stated that children of a plural marriage would be considered legitimate if born before January 1, 1883. The plural wife, however, still had no legal standing.

Brigham Young believed the Mormon position on polygamy was based on the freedom of religion as constitutionally protected by the First Amendment. In the mid-1870s, Elder George Reynolds was convicted in district court of polygamy under the Morrill Act. President Young, hoping to legally resolve the issue, urged Reynolds to appeal his conviction to the Supreme Court. In *Reynolds v. United States,* Elder Reynolds argued that it was his religious duty to enter into multiple marriages.[12] Chief Justice Morrison Waite responded: "Religious duty was not a suitable defense to a criminal indictment." The Court ruled that although the First Amendment did not allow Congress to legislate against religious *opinions,* it did, indeed, allow Congress to legislate against certain *actions.*

George Q. Cannon, territorial representative in Washington, as well as member of the Church's Quorum of the Twelve and brother of Angus Munn Cannon, stated in response to the *Reynolds* decision the same *social* rationale for polygamy that the Mormon women themselves had made in an 1870 petition to Congress:

> *Our crime has been: We married women instead of seducing them, we reared children instead of destroying them, we desired to exclude from the land prostitution, bastardy and infanticide. . . . If George Reynolds is to be punished, let the world know the facts. . . . Let it be published to the four corners of the earth that in this land of liberty, the most blessed and glorious upon which the sun shines, the law is swiftly invoked to punish religion, but justice goes limping and blindfolded in pursuit of crime.*[13]

Gunfights, pillagings, house burnings, and other forms of violence against Mormons and their property gave way to lampoon, satire, scorn, and harangue. Cartoons were prevalent, many of which ridiculed Mormon women. In his book about traveling through the West, *Roughing It*, Mark Twain lampoons the Book of Mormon, calling it "chloroform in print." He includes a cartoon showing Brigham Young in an enormous bed with a row of women on either side of him. Twain characterizes Mormon women as

> *poor, ungainly, and pathetically "homely" creatures. . . . The man that marries one of them has done an act of Christian charity which entitles him to the kindly applause of mankind, not their harsh censure—and the man that marries sixty of them has done a deed of openhanded generosity so sublime the nation should stand uncovered in his presence and worship in silence!*[14]

Despite the humor or the outrage of those outside the Church, Mormon plural marriage was essentially puritanical. Adultery was punished with excommunication, if not on occasion by "blood atonement," that is, the deliberate taking of another's life, both for revenge and to save the other's soul for entry to the heavenly spheres. In the Church's view, God had introduced the patriarchal order of marriage in order to incarnate little souls waiting to be born, bringing them into this world—as many as possible—to swell the ranks of the Mormon priesthood.

Among the women there were some apostates that fed the public's appetite for scandal. One of the most famous was Ann Eliza Young, a forward ex-wife of Brigham Young, who traveled the United States speaking to women's groups against polygamy as a revolting slavery and suggesting that many of the marriages involved incest. It is thought that her lectures and later her testimony before Congress in the 1870s may have influenced the passage of the Poland Act. Another apostate was Fanny Stenhouse, who wrote the popular book, *Tell It All*, and who lectured in the eastern cities about the evils of polygamy and theocracy. Both Fanny and her husband left the Church over Brigham Young's politics and what they believed to be his polygamous immorality.

There are stories of loving sister-wives supporting and caring for each other, such as in the household of Milford Shipp. Wife Margaret took care of wife Ellis's children and sent Ellis money so that she could study for her MD degree in the East. And there are stories of using women as commodities, as mere baby-producing machines. Lucy Walker, a plural wife of Apostle Heber C. Kimball, notes in her diary, "There was not any love in the union between myself and Kimball, for it was the principle of plural marriage we were trying to establish, a great and glorious true principle."[15] Apparently Kimball didn't see the relationship as quite so great and glorious, for he commented, "I think no more of taking another wife than I do of buying a cow."[16]

In 1882 the Edmunds Act stated that polygamy was a felony, punishable by five years in prison and a $500 fine. Because it was difficult to prove actual marriage without civil registration, the act stated that cohabitation was punishable by six months in prison and a $300 fine.[17] Polygamous men were barred from public office, from serving on juries, and disenfranchised. The government was even threatening to confiscate the Mormons' Salt Lake Temple, which was still under construction.

The act also inaugurated the era of "the raid." Federal marshals were all over Utah trying to catch "cohabs," if not in their beds, at least in their houses. Government agents were peeping into windows, bribing children to reveal family relationships, disguising themselves in common clothes to try to encourage gossip. They hired "spotters" and offered $10 and $20 bounties to catch a Saint. And with such a bounty, there were apostates and Gentiles called "skunks" and "Mormon-eaters" willing to go "cohab hunting" for the feds—even then "feds" was the name given the U.S. marshals. The Saints went into hiding; some of the families fled to Canada, others started colonies in Mexico. Not unlike slavery's Underground Railroad of an earlier era, they developed secret codes to send warnings from town to town of the advance of the marshals. Because of his prominence in Church affairs and his family connections, the marshals were particularly interested in grabbing the polygamous Angus Munn Cannon.

President Taylor was adamant that the Saints must maintain the practice of polygamy. As the government raids increased the pressure on the community, Taylor became correspondingly defiant. At an April 1884 conference of the priesthood, the president asked for all monogamists serving as ward bishops or stake presidents to either find themselves a second wife or resign their positions.[18] Shortly after, the president went "underground" at a friend's ranch, administering Church matters from his hiding place.

It is difficult to understand why an intelligent, ambitious young woman, having just finished an extensive education and rising in her career, would secretly sneak off to the Endowment House to be sealed for eternity to a man old enough to be her father—a man who was already married to three women, had seventeen children of his own plus four stepchildren, and who was Suspect Number One on the federal agents' "most wanted" list.[19] Surely Mattie could see that ultimately there would be no compromise possible with the law, and that she would never be able to live openly with her husband. But Mattie's actions reveal a passionate, irrational side of her nature, one that was not always in balance with the ambitions she had pursued with such determination. That she was desperately in love is clear from the letters she wrote to Angus, which he kept and which are now in the LDS archives. And her letters also show that she believed that polygamy was a revelation of God's will, that in their plural marriage, she and Angus were living what the Saints referred to as "the principle." It was this strong religious belief that allowed her to deal with the anger and pain of jealousy that she fought in herself, and the disappointments, both personal and professional, that an illegal and problematic marriage would soon force upon her.

CHAPTER 5

No one but the Church authorities who performed the Endowment House ceremony for the couple knew about Mattie and Angus's marriage—not even her parents. The need for secrecy was paramount. The federal agents were aware of Angus's polygamous marriages to his three wives, but they did not know about Mattie. At least not at first. Mattie continued her work at the Deseret Hospital; she even wrote to her college friend Barbara Replogle a month after her marriage: "Truly the fates seem against all attempts of love and matrimony on my part. I fear I am doomed to maidenhood."[1] Why Mattie would lie to her friend is not clear. Perhaps she was afraid her mail would be intercepted, or perhaps she just didn't want her non-Mormon friend to know of the situation she had gotten herself into. Even later, when Mattie was well along in a pregnancy, she kept up her deceit: "Barb, you will hurt yourself laughing when I relate to you some of my experiences. They have had me married to one of the Mormon leaders, and arraigned me before the Grand Jury to answer to the charge of being an associate in polygamy—of course I was acquitted."[2]

The U.S. attorney for the Utah Territory, W. H. Dickson, was determined to catch the Church leaders in polygamy, or if that could not be proved, in cohabitation. Dickson hired Samuel Gilson's detective agency, and almost immediately the detective caught Angus. In May 1885, Angus was sentenced to six months in prison and a $300 fine for "lascivious cohabitation"

with his second wife, Amanda, and his third wife, Clara. During his trial earlier in the year, the government called Clara, his
twenty-four-year-old son George, and his nineteen-year-old son
John to testify as to their living arrangements. The witnesses
described Angus's large house as containing two separate apart-
ments with kitchen, parlor, and bedroom for each wife, Clara
and Amanda. Angus lived in the house also, and he divided his
time between them. He also provided for his first wife Sarah in
a separate home. He took his meals alternately with each wife
and those children still remaining at home. Angus stated to the
court that he had tried to avoid prosecution by providing separate living quarters for his three wives and by being able to
swear forgoing any sexual contact with them. The court ruled
that the government's inability to prove sexual relations was
irrelevant. The defense argued that Angus and his three wives
were married prior to the 1882 Edmunds Act. The act said that
it was to apply to marriages performed after the date of enact-
ment. However this did not affect the charge of cohabitation.
The court defined cohabitation as including "living together as
members of one family, a consorting in social intercourse, and
eating and lodging together. They need not occupy the same
bed, but there must be an equivalent intimacy."[3]

The U.S. attorney had heard rumors of Angus's fourth marriage. Two employees of Deseret Hospital were called to testify if
Angus was married to Mattie or if he had ever spent the night at
the hospital, presumably with Mattie. Neither of the employees
was aware of a marriage or of Angus's spending the night. The
initial warrant had included Mattie as a possible suspect, but she
couldn't be found. She had eluded the officers looking for her
at the Deseret Hospital. The *Deseret News* reported that during
a brief recess, Commissioner McKay offered to furnish Angus
with a subpoena if he would go and serve it on Miss Hughes.
"Needless to state that this generous tender was declined."[4]

Reluctant to submit his wives and his sons to further humiliation in the court, Angus pleaded guilty. When Judge Charles S. Zane asked him if he had anything to say, Angus responded:

> *I can only say that I have used the utmost of my power to honor my God, my family, and my country. In eating with my children day by day, and showing impartiality in meeting with them around the board with the mother who was wont to wait upon them, I was unconscious of any crime. . . . My record is before my country; the conscience of my heart is visible to the God who created me, and the rectitude that has marked my life and conduct with this people bears me up to receive such a sentence as your Honor shall see fit to impose upon me.*[5]

The spectators in the court applauded loudly, but Judge Zane did not consider this statement as contrition. Although the law allowed the judge some leniency in sentencing, Angus received the full penalty.

The ruling that sexual relations were not necessary to prove cohabitation was the basis of an appeal to the Supreme Court the following December by Angus's lawyer, Franklin S. Richards, while Angus waited in prison. The court upheld the government's position that living in the same house and taking meals with each of the women was sufficient to indicate cohabitation.

Angus's journal for this period is obliquely discreet, but it also reveals a stalwart and almost arrogant attitude regarding his arrest. He mentions that there was a farewell party for him in the assembly hall of the Fourteenth Ward, and that the tabernacle choir serenaded him the night before his departure. The buggy procession through Salt Lake City to the state penitentiary the next day, May 9, 1885, must have looked to the townspeople like a parade. The city marshal, having just taken dinner at Angus's house, accompanied him in the buggy, along with Angus's lawyer and friend, Franklin S. Richards; Angus's wife Amanda; and sons Jesse and Quayle. After them followed a second buggy with his son Angus and his wife Clara and daughter Alice. Behind them followed "Sister Mattie P. Hughes" with Angus's daughter Ann and a matron from the Deseret Hospital. After them came another buggy with sons George, Lewis, and Clarence; then followed his friends, Brother Orson P. Arnold and Andrew Smith; and finally, bringing up the rear, Brother Elias Morris.[6]

Angus's journal entry from the penitentiary the next day states: "I thank God I am counted worthy to represent our cause in this prison. Friends and family came bringing flowers and fruit and other comforts." A week later is Angus's birthday: "Friends and family brought a birthday cake and fruit and flowers, etc., candies and clean clothes." Some days later he notes that ladies from the Anti-Polygamy Society brought flowers, which he declined, saying his wives had already brought plenty of flowers. He is even let out for a day to take care of some business. He notes in his journal that he spent the day with his family and was back at the prison by seven.[7] Doubtless, the prison was administered by fellow Saints.

During 1885, as the signs of her pregnancy began to show, Mattie knew she would have to go into hiding to protect both her husband and herself. Not only must she hide because her pregnancy would give away the proof of her polygamous marriage, but also, because she was a doctor, she was wanted as a witness. She had assisted at many births of children of polygamous marriages, and the federal agents were after her to testify against the fathers. There was a $200 bond on her head to force her to appear as a witness. As she said in a letter to her friend Barbara: "To me it is a serious matter to be the cause of sending to jail a father upon whom a lot of little children are dependent, whether those children were begotten by the same or different mothers—the fact remains they all have little mouths that *must be fed*.[8]

Shortly after Angus's incarceration, Mattie went into hiding at the home of Samuel Woolley, friends in Grantsville, Utah. Here she gave birth to her daughter, Elizabeth Rachel, on September 13, 1885. Unfortunately Mattie developed puerperal fever, a common, but dangerous condition of parturition that she had earlier warned of to her students in her classes at the hospital. Samuel's wife nursed her back to health, and after some months Mattie moved with her baby to the home of John Woolley in Centerville. According to Elizabeth McCrimmon's manuscript, mother and daughter traveled to Centerville in a sheep wagon during a blizzard. Upon arrival the baby was almost dead, and Mattie blew into her baby's lungs to get her breathing again.

Angus was released from prison in December 1885, but he still had to live "underground." Freedom didn't stop government harassment. In August 1886, he wrote in his journal: "Marshals surrounded my Bluff-Dale farm house, looking for Mr. Cannon."[9] By November he was carrying a gun; he spent the next two years hiding at his son George's home.

The Supreme Court's 1885 decision that proof of sexual relations was not necessary to the charge of cohabitation unleashed an era of Mormon-bashing that U.S. marshals carried out with seeming glee. Court dockets all over Utah were clogged with cases of polygamy and cohabitation. On March 6, 1885, over two thousand women gathered in the Salt Lake Theatre to protest the government's treatment of their husbands and to send a letter to President Grover Cleveland, objecting to the ruthless attitude of the territorial officials.

Passage of the Edmunds-Tucker Act in 1887 took away the women's right to vote, a right that they had held since 1870,

and it gave the prosecutors even more ammunition by repeal-
ing the right of a wife or husband to refuse to testify against a
spouse. A wife who refused to cooperate or who lied to protect
her husband was charged with perjury, and any polygamous
or "cohab" suspect could be jailed until a trial date. Between
1885 and 1889, the government had collected almost $103,500 in
fines and had begun seizing and liquidating Church holdings.
Church leaders would claim that by 1890, thirteen hundred
Saints had been imprisoned.[10] In many instances their Mormon
brethren regarded the prisoners as martyrs, and when the latter were released, they were met at the prison gates with brass
bands and escorted to their homes in parade.[11]

One of the arguments the Saints made in defense of polygamy was that in Salt Lake City there had been no prostitution
until the Gentiles arrived. Incensed at their treatment by the
government and at the Gentiles' disparagement of their sacred
principle of polygamy as simply licentious behavior, some LDS
members determined to use prostitution to entrap their enemies. They were on the lookout to catch one of the prosecutors
in a "compromising" situation. The *Salt Lake Tribune* reported
on November 22, 1885, that one Deputy Vandercook "is charged
with lewd and lascivious conduct with one Mrs. A. J. Field."[12] At
one point the Salt Lake City police opened a brothel in the city
with secret compartments for spying; prostitutes were brought
in and the madam sent enticing notes to the government agents.
While off duty the police took turns manning the peepholes and
caught Assistant U.S. Attorney S. H. Lewis in the act. Lewis was
found guilty of "lewd and lascivious conduct," but on appeal
was let off. U.S. Attorney Varian, defending Lewis, stated about
the police conduct: "I do not believe any American jury would
believe such infamous scoundrels, who have crawled to the
threshold of the house of the harlot."[13] The judge agreed with
Varian, determining the police had committed a crime to induce

others to commit a crime. One of the policemen was later tried and convicted for "conspiracy to open a house of ill fame."[14]

One outsider who was outraged by the government's treatment of the Saints under the Edmunds Act was the civil rights lawyer Belva Lockwood. Lockwood had supported the Utah women's desire to join Susan B. Anthony's National Woman Suffrage Association (NWSA) and was appalled at the rudeness with which at first some of the easterners treated the Mormon women. But beyond her concern for the suffrage issues, Lockwood was adamant that the anti-Mormon legislation was unconstitutional in that it permitted illegal searches and seizures—allowing an agent to break into a suspect's home or climb through a window in the middle of the night. She firmly believed that the Edmunds Act and later the Edmunds-Tucker Act were not passed to preserve the morality of the nation, but simply to destroy religious freedom.

While the Saints plotted to catch a government agent in their municipal brothel, Lockwood tried a different tack to embarrass the government: She proposed to apply the terms of the Edmunds Act outside Utah, hopefully to show the country the implications of such injustice when applied in another state. Working with a New York LDS lawyer, together they hoped to prosecute men who had left their wives to live with another woman. She planned to force the wife to testify against her husband. Unfortunately for the Saints, Lockwood's plan failed: She couldn't find cases that involved prominent people, and the ones she could find failed to stir up interest.[15]

In 1855, while working as a young missionary in Delaware, Angus fell in love with Amanda Mousley. He wished to marry her and Amanda returned his feelings. Angus had converted the Mousley family to Mormonism and made arrangements for them to immigrate to Utah. Brigham Young approved Angus's

Angus Munn Cannon's home with two of his wives

request to marry Amanda in 1858, but insisted that the young man marry Amanda's older sister, Sarah, as well. Young also insisted that Angus marry Sarah before Amanda, thus making Sarah the first wife—and later in U.S. law, the only legal wife. Apparently this wasn't at all what Angus had had in mind, but as a loyal subject of the Church, he complied. The three lived in apparent harmony, and the sisters remained close, even though Angus preferred Amanda. Amanda was the wife he presented to the public as if she were the first wife, the hostess of the many social affairs arising from his position as president of the huge Salt Lake Stake, an area that covered several counties as well as the city. Angus's journal shows that he loved Amanda very deeply. He and Amanda lived together, and because her health was frail, he helped her in many ways. He never forgot her birthday, and he never forgot to give her her weekly allowance. He notes in his journal that he would rise early in order to light a fire in the room so that Amanda would not be cold.[16] Sarah lived in a separate house. Amanda gave birth to ten children over the years, Sarah to six.

Then in 1875, Angus married Clarissa—Clara—Mason, a widow with two children of her own and two adopted children. Perhaps this marriage was an example of the humanitarian side of polygamy. Men were often called by the Church authorities to marry certain women—much as Young had called Angus to marry Amanda's sister because she was older. Polygamy offered protection and a certain amount of financial support to a single woman, a woman like Sarah, who perhaps could not have attracted a husband on her own, or to a widowed woman like Clara. And, of course, such marriages allowed for the further production of little Saints. Angus and Clara had three children, of which only one survived. Clara and her children lived for a while in Angus's house with Amanda and her family—as she described to the court—but later moved into her own home.

Mattie's medical practice was completely disrupted by the need to hide from the federal marshals during her pregnancy and the months that she needed to regain her health after her daughter's birth. And even then, she could not practice in the open. By this time the government officials were aware of her marriage. She hated living undercover, dodging warrants, always afraid of being caught. Her letters reveal that she felt she was being asked to sacrifice too much to protect Angus, but still she didn't want him to be arrested again. She wrote to him in March of 1886: "I grow heartily sick and disgusted with it [polygamy]."[17] It was at this time that Mattie determined she would go abroad to England, where she could visit her mother's relatives. It meant, of course, that her professional career would be put on hold again, but both she and her daughter would be out of reach of the government; she could not be called as a witness against Angus or against any other suspected polygamist.

Mattie firmly believed that the principle of plural marriage was a divine revelation. Angus's three wives were much older than she and most of their children already grown. Probably she did not see his other wives as rivals for the physical expression of his love. She doesn't express jealousy toward them; indeed her letters suggest that she is concerned about them, particularly about Clara, whom she obviously likes and with whom she corresponds. Being an emotional young woman, she had no doubt suffered being separated from her husband when their baby was born. Her letters indicate that she needed to know that she was the most important in his affections. And yet, as Mattie was making her arrangements to leave for Europe to protect him from being arrested on her account, how difficult it must have been for her to accept that a few days before her departure, Angus married a fifth wife, Maria Bennion, a woman six months younger than she.

CHAPTER 6

According to recollections of a descendant of the Cannon family, Angus Munn Cannon was "active, alert, and scrupulously careful in his personal habits. He delighted in cleanliness in both person and attire. . . . With his exact carriage, his handsome face, and attired in his habitual black Prince Albert suit, high silk hat and cane, he everywhere commanded attention and respect."[1] A grandson relates an anecdote about Angus's authority in the community:

> *Angus went out in his fine Prince Albert coat and hat and tried to flag down the trolley. Unknown to Angus, the trolley company had recently changed that route to an express line, so the train failed to stop. Immediately Angus went inside and called the president of the Utah Traction Company and told him to make sure that all trains stopped for him. . . . From then on the trolley did stop for Angus, wherever and whenever he flagged it down.*[2]

Mattie and Angus's daughter, Elizabeth Rachel, described Angus as "handsome, magnetic, with a gift of language. [His] chief characteristic was his spirituality. He put his devotion to the church above everything." She went on to say that her mother, being strongly spiritual herself, was attracted to that quality in Angus.[3]

Angus Munn Cannon, ca. 1890

An example of Angus's spirituality is his report of a vision that happened after he had left prison. He relates to a friend that he heard a voice say to him:

> *Angus, it is your privilege to appear before the Lord, and I immediately looked and beheld him, apparently about 30 rods distant. I was crouching down at the time but was as wide awake as it was possible for me to be—but I saw his profile down to his waist. . . . I undertook to arise and go to him but dared not approach him, and said: "My God! Who can appear before Him." I imagined he would say: How have you used my name and what use have you made of my Priesthood? When I thought of my many light speeches and the manner in which I had striven to embellish my remarks, in addressing people as His servant, circumlocuting around the truths given of Him as witness his sermon on the mount, I was unable to go to him.*[4]

Angus's personality seems to have been a combination of authoritative self-importance in temporal affairs and profound spiritual humility before the divine.

That Angus loved Mattie is clear from the entry he wrote in his journal the day she told him of her decision to leave the country: "I am told friend wants to go to England and I consent. . . . I leave her tonight with the saddest heart I ever felt."[5] He expressed great joy on receiving her first letters from England, and during that summer at a family picnic, "my mind wandered to those far away and I thought: how sad I cannot acknowledge and meet all I so dearly love."[6] And later, "You have been loved as much as woman has been, are, and yet will be loved, as only a true heart is capable of loving you."[7]

If, as Elizabeth Rachel says, Angus put his devotion to the Church above everything—which would mean putting the Church above his love for Mattie—then we might assume that his marriage to Maria Bennion was to carry out the wishes of the Church authorities. Maria's father was an intimate friend of Angus, and Angus had business dealings with Maria's brothers. Perhaps, at twenty-nine, the men felt that Maria was getting too old to catch herself a husband. One wonders, however, why Angus would not be more cognizant of Mattie's feelings at such a critical time, or why both he and Maria's father would put yet another woman in a position where she must hide from the government officers. Maria spent the next several years living in Logan, Utah. Although she never lived with Angus, they had four children together.

Of course we can't know what explanation must have passed between Mattie and Angus, but the marriage to Maria obviously didn't diminish Mattie's love for him. However, her letters do, on occasion, show her jealousy, but it is as if jealousy is yet another way to show her love for him. Obviously Mattie and Angus had had a fight about his marriage to Maria. She wrote to him: "I wish we could look at the divine part of these things *only* . . . but with so much earthiness in our nature (mine) this is not always easily accomplished. . . . You recollect I had not reached this point when you left, I mean the forgiving part."[8]

Maria Bennion was a large, buxom woman, known for being able to wrestle a calf to the ground. Mattie referred to her in her letters as "big Maria," and signed some of her own as "your *little* Maria."

According to her daughter's manuscript, when Mattie left with baby Lizzie for New York from where she would travel to England, she was recognized at the train station and had to hurry to another location so as not to get caught. Her luggage was left behind in the rush, and she never got it back. Not withstanding the necessity of leaving Angus, and of once again having to put her career on hold, Mattie was obviously excited about taking this trip. She wrote Angus from the ship, the SS

Wyoming, "everything is lovely with us," that her "peevishness" appeared to be gone, and she had begun to feel herself again.[9]

Mattie made contact with the LDS English missionaries in Liverpool, the headquarters of the Mormon British and European missions. Then she moved on to Birmingham, where she had an uncle. She found in England several other "undergrounders"— Mormons in exile. All of them were using false names in their correspondence back to Utah. When she met her uncle, she told him her name was Martha Munn, and that she had married a widower. She wrote to Angus under several assumed names in the course of her exile, one of which was Maria, her middle name. It is curious why she would choose to use that name: "How I despise the name *Maria*—but I never did admire it before I had any occasion to be jealous."[10]

Mattie's time in Birmingham became more and more difficult for her. She couldn't stand her uncle's wife, who screamed at her children and drank her "half-a-pint-of-four-penny" several times a day. And her aunt's children deliberately terrified Lizzie. Lizzie was sick, and Mattie realized she had to get out of the unhealthy, polluted city. She took Lizzie and moved to Wolverton, a lovely country town near Stratford-on-Avon, where she also had relatives. She wrote Angus that Lizzie was immediately better after the move, but she couldn't resist commenting "perhaps at this very moment you are basking in the smiles of your *young* Maria."

Mattie thought she might be pregnant, but it turned out to be a resurgence of the uterine problems she incurred with the birth of her daughter. However, for a time she speculated that she and Maria Bennion might give birth at the same time. Again she lashed out in jealousy: "I'll dwell no longer on this subject or it will produce the same effect on me that Joseph F. said the Federal Officials of Utah would produce on Hell when they presented themselves at its gates—that is 'make itself vomit sick.'"[11]

Although Mattie was glad to be in the country, she was disgusted by the lower-class English who surrounded her:

England is horrid to me; or rather the mode of living among the lower classes is dreadful. We in Utah live like kings compared to the people here . . . yet this is heaven compared to the beggary and crime of the cities. . . . No one here half eats but drink like fish. You have no idea to what excess they carry it, and constantly guzzling so many malt preparations down. . . . I am paying a fair price for board and lodgings and am fed mainly on rusty bacon and "bread & scrape," and not enough of that.[12]

Both she and Lizzie were not well for several months in England, and at one point Lizzie accidentally drank some ammonia and almost died. Mattie treated Lizzie herself, but she also sent for her fellow churchmen to come and administer the healing rituals to the child. As the months wore on, Mattie became more and more despondent, and began to blame Angus for the misery of her exile. Her moods were highly changeable; at times her letters castigated him and at times they were full of love for him. And at times they were sarcastic. Referring to the fact that she was no longer even a fourth wife, she wrote: "I assure you, taking the great plan into consideration, a quarter section, aye! even less is preferable to none at all of your precious self." The "great plan" is the polygamy that Mattie was constantly justifying to herself as God's will. She would confess her jealousy, then castigate herself for feeling jealous. She told Angus that he was too much of a polygamist or "is progressing finely, that way, while I am playing the ass over here, am wondering what the Lord thinks of the mess of us."[13]

She was dependent on Angus for financial help. In July 1886, she wrote him that there was not the slightest opportunity for her to practice her profession in England. The people were too poor to buy their medicines, let alone pay a physician. However she assured him she would be economical. Then in another letter she assured him she would repay him *"every cent,* interest and all."[14] For a while she lived with another woman in exile, a "Mrs. Hull," who also was hiding her identity.[15] The woman had an infant near Lizzie's age, and for a while it seemed beneficial that the two women live together, but ultimately Mattie wanted to get away from her.

Mattie visited Shakespeare's home in Stratford-on-Avon and other castles and monuments near Wolverton. Excited as she was about the specific monuments, everywhere she went it was with a sickly child clinging to her and whom most of the time she had to carry everywhere. She explored London and went to Wales to seek out her father's relatives. Her Birmingham uncle read one of her letters and discovered that she was in a polygamous marriage. He became extremely obnoxious, calling her an imposter, her illness a sham, that she was connected to "one of *those things* out there"—one of "those things" apparently meaning Angus.

In March 1887, Angus married thirty-eight-year-old Johanna Danielson, another woman who apparently had not found a husband. Since Mattie's subsequent letters don't mention this marriage, perhaps Angus hadn't told her, or perhaps she dismissed the event with her comment: "I don't think you will find me lashing myself into jealous rages if you see fit to take additional young wives for eternity and to propagate the species, as I have come to the conclusion that I am totally unfit for the work, and must be content to see others do it."[16] Apparently Angus's inclination to "put his devotion to the Church above everything," was expressed in his duty to procreate for the further glory of God and His Church.

Mattie visited London hospitals to learn the English procedures of patient care. She introduced herself as an American nurse and was shocked to see that at one hospital inexperienced boys were employed to care for the patients. At another she took Lizzie and inspected the pediatric section. After observing the treatment of children, she commented to Angus that whenever she needed to make Lizzie behave, she just told her she would take her to the "hospital man." The threat snapped the child out of whatever complaints.

Lewis, the son of Angus and his first wife, Amanda, was sent to England to be a missionary, and Mattie met him in Liverpool. Lewis was a very provincial and rather naïve young man, and Mattie took him in hand. The two traveled together to Paris, and Mattie was enchanted by the city: "[W]herever the eye rests in this great center can be seen the impress of intellect—to wander through its collections of art—its palaces of departed monarchs—its halls of pleasure, or drive through the gardens and boulevards . . . has been a period of enchantment such as I never thought to experience." She wrote Angus that whatever sadness she had felt in England, "this *surely* most beautiful city in the world . . . has compensated for *all*."[17]

Typical of Mattie's letters, they expound on her love for Angus, her delight in being his wife, her excitement over her experiences abroad—and then plunge to despair, rejecting his protestations of love, and hating her surroundings. Sometimes these swings are brought on by the health problems that plagued her the entire time of her exile, as well as her worry over her daughter's frail health; sometimes they seem to be a reaction to the people and places around her. After the delights of Paris, she accompanied Lewis to Switzerland, where he was to be stationed to do his missionary work, and where he had to learn German. She stayed with a Mormon acquaintance who was Swiss, but she couldn't stand Switzerland. She couldn't understand the language, and hence fell into a depression. She wrote to Angus: "[W]ere it not for her [Lizzie] and the religion of our God I should never want to see Salt Lake again but seek some other spot and strive to forget what a failure my life has been." She dug at him about his happy family in Utah, envious that he had the love of his wide family there. Angus thought that Mattie should come back to America. She rebutted: "[B]ut [you] express no word of joy at my release. You are happy with those you love—what care you?"[18]

Angus answered these letters with renewed avowals of love: "You may doubt it with your own soul, but you are loved by the man you have gone through everything for and sacrificed everything on earth for."[19] To such declarations, Mattie would beg for forgiveness for having doubted him and having said hurtful things to him——and the cycle of jealousy and doubt followed by apologies and contrition would start over again.

Mattie's exile abroad finally ended in December 1887 as she sailed from Liverpool on the SS *Arizona*, bound for New York. She was concerned to get medical help for both herself and Lizzie, who was showing signs of a serious urinary tract problem. She knew she wouldn't be able to return yet to Utah because the prosecutions there were in full force. She was even wary of what might happen when she landed in New York, since she was not sure if her identity might have been revealed to the authorities. Still, she was happy to be returning to America, "Even now I am happy at the thought I am breathing American air."[20] She was hoping to find a letter waiting for her in New York, and was delighted to see instead that Angus had come to meet her.

CHAPTER 7

Mattie's exile was by no means over. Utah had become a virtual dystopia. The judicial crusade was continuing in full swing and had spread to Mormon settlements in Arizona and Idaho. When the prisons became too crowded, the convicted cohabs were shipped two thousand miles away to Detroit. There was a $500 reward posted for the arrest of Angus's brother, George Q. Cannon, and a $300 reward for the Church's president, John Taylor, Angus's uncle. Just as Mattie was leaving for England, George Q. was caught in Nevada and brought back by military escort to Utah for trial. He jumped bail, forfeiting $45,000, and again went underground until he turned himself in twenty months later and was sent to prison. President Taylor managed to evade capture, but his health failed and he died in July 1887, still in hiding at a friend's ranch.

The Saints fought back against the federal agents, employing "spotters" who followed the marshals around and warned the neighborhoods. Many in the rural areas refused to sell food to the agents. In September 1885, a group of angry Mormons attacked the homes of U.S. Attorneys Dickson and Varian and U.S. Commissioner McKay. The group hurled jars of human excrement through the windows, which broke on the walls and carpets.[1]

The 1887 Edmunds-Tucker Act had closed some loopholes in the previous antipolygamy acts, and this time set out a strict system of enforcement. Among other things the act once more officially dissolved the Church of Jesus Christ of Latter-day Saints as a legal corporation, disbanded the territorial militia, abolished women's suffrage, required wives to testify against their husbands, and required any man wishing to hold office to take an antipolygamy loyalty oath. The abolition of suffrage applied to all Utah women, LDS or not, but apparently this was acceptable to the Gentile women, since it reduced the political power of the Mormons. Schools were placed under the control of the federal territorial Supreme Court, and all marriages required civil certification in the probate courts. Although the 1862 Morrill Act had required the escheat of Church property valued in excess of $50,000, the act had not been enforced, partly because of the Civil War, but also because Congress didn't appropriate the funds to carry out prosecutions. As a precaution, however, in the 1870s Brigham Young had begun transferring ownership of much Church property to his own name as a private individual, and to the names of other Church leaders. This process was continued under President Taylor. Immediately after the Edmunds-Tucker Act was passed, the federal receiver confiscated any Church property not in private ownership, renting some of it back to the Saints. One such rental property was the entire Temple Square with the unfinished temple, the tabernacle, and other Church buildings. The receiver then went after the private property that had been transferred from Church ownership, maintaining the transfer was a ruse. The Saints argued in the Supreme Court that such confiscations were an unconstitutional abridgement of property rights. They lost. On the political front as well as the legal, the non-Mormon Liberal Party was gaining power. The Liberals had captured the elections of Ogden, and in 1890 they won control in the municipal elections in Salt Lake City. The government had disenfranchised all Utah women and any man who was unwilling to swear obedience to antipolygamy laws. Hence Mormon defeat was inevitable. On election night Gentiles thronged the streets as the returns came in, and the city flamed with bonfires of celebration. The shocked Saints faced the impending devastation of their Kingdom.[2]

After spending several days together in New York, Mattie and Lizzie traveled to Michigan, where Mattie had attended medical school, while Angus returned to Utah. On his way he stopped in Richmond, Missouri, to visit David Whitmer. Whitmer was in his nineties, a member of the RLDS Church that had broken with Brigham Young back in Nauvoo. He was the only survivor of the three men who purportedly had witnessed the Book of Mormon with Joseph Smith. Whitmer swore to Angus that he had indeed seen the gold tablets on which the Book of Mormon was written and that the angel had taken away. A month later the old man was dead. Angus didn't need Whitmer's testimony to reaffirm his faith, but it was important to him to be the last man to hear the words from the actual witness.[3]

Mattie took the train to Algonac in St. Clair County, Michigan, where she could stay with friends she had made at the time that she worked there. It was January, the temperature twenty degrees below, and she was worried that Lizzie's cough would turn into pneumonia. She wrote Angus not only about her concerns for Lizzie, but also lamented her sense of homelessness, that she was sick and tired of "knocking about" ever since she had married. "If you have one scintilla of desire to make me happy on this earth, then I say for pity sakes try and provide me with a home of *my own* when I reach the Rocky Mts."[4] Angus wanted her to return to Utah even though the move would mean she would still have to go into hiding. He sent her train tickets. She replied that she needed to take Lizzie to the doctor in Ann Arbor, but it was too cold to travel there for a while, and that she, herself, should stay for some months in Ann Arbor to consult with her doctor and try to cure the uterine problems that persisted.

From Algonac she wrote him a long letter full of ambivalence over her situation, telling him of the marriages she had encountered among the Gentiles, where "the wife and mother is proud and happy in the devotion of a noble husband, while he in turn is equally contented and happy in the possession of the partner he has chosen for life; while at *home* in each other's association, is where their greatest joys are centered." She compared this with her own marriage of "a few stolen interviews thoroughly tinctured with the *dread of discovery.*" Perhaps she was also thinking of her parents' monogamous marriage, or that of her older sister Mary Elizabeth, who married James Neeley in 1878, and remained his only wife. She went on to say, "I am thankful that God so ordained my destiny to embrace the celestial principle of marriage when I did. . . . Had my movements towards marriage been left or deferred until the present time, and that I had merely human instincts to guide me, I should have given the whole plural system a wide berth." Further, she wrote: "[W]ere it not for daily petitions to God for strength, the adversary [Satan] would make me feel and believe it is really a condition of degradation instead of one of honorable wifehood. If you only knew the subterfuges one has to resort to in order to make any movements appear reasonable to sensible people with whom I meet, while occupying the position I do, you would not wonder at a sense of degradation stealing over me at times." But then she hurried to reassure him. "I would rather spend one hour in your society, than a whole life time with any other man I know of."[5]

The conflict in Mattie's nature kept surfacing in the letters that followed. She teased him—or perhaps she was digging at him—when she wrote about how cold it was in St. Clair, nothing like the wonderful warm summer she spent there in her student days, dreaming of a former suitor: "Twas here I used to compose love letters and dream of 'Liolin' in his southern home—and of fame and happiness in years to come—and in response I would receive proud letters from my hero, with bunches of jasmine and moss roses and 'forget-me-nots' all withered, but with a lingering fragrance of the 'sunny south.' " And as usual, she followed the statement with "I can only be reconciled to all this change in one way, that is to be near you and know that you love me." She finished the letter, commenting, "If, after a marriage covering a period of nearly four years, a man can't provide a wife and child with a *home*, he isn't worth having."[6]

Mattie's desire for a home of her own was paramount, and she mentioned it in every letter she wrote Angus from Michigan. Angus still urged her to return to Utah, and she replied that she had considered coming home undercover but had decided she would not. "I would rather be a stranger in a strange land and be able to hold my head up among my fellow beings than to be a sneaking captive at home."[7] Angus complained to her that he, too, was homeless, because he had to hide out at his son's house. She responded angrily that he didn't know what *homeless* meant. "I often wonder," she wrote, "*why* I have been subjected to the life I have led for the past three and a half years. It is certainly one of three things. Earning a 'big' reward, atoning for past delinquencies, or else because I am a *damned fool*."[8] Complaint, followed by penitence and contrition, followed by justification of her life as God's intent had become a pattern she would continue to live out for years.

When Mattie finally got to Ann Arbor in the spring, she found that the specialist she wanted to see for her uterine problems was dying. She decided against consulting about her problem with anyone else, but she did have Lizzie examined. She discovered the reasons for Lizzie's nervousness and behavioral problems were that the child had an infected bladder. She was

counseled to do nothing about the problem for a while as a bladder stone had not yet developed, and perhaps one wouldn't.
Mattie hired a woman to take care of Lizzie so that she could
have some time to study in the new university library and visit
the art galleries. Mornings she attended lectures, and she wrote
Angus that she felt like a college student again. She lamented
that she hadn't spent the winter in Ann Arbor, where she could
have attended the university, rather than in Algonac.

From Ann Arbor mother and daughter went on to Chicago
where Mattie was looking forward to meeting her college friend
Barbara Replogle. For Mattie, Barbara represented a contact
with the eager dreams and ambitions of her earlier years. As
Mattie suggested in her letter to Angus, she did once imagine a
future of fame for herself. Shortly after her marriage, she wrote
to Barbara: "[L]et us not waste our talents in the cauldron of
modern nothingness—but strive to become women of intellect
and strive to do some *little good* while we live in this protracted
gleam called life."[9] She told Barbara that what leisure time she
had would be devoted to literature, and she wished she could
discuss the "heroes of literature" with her.[10] While in England
she wrote Barbara about the empty life of the young people
around her. "[T]hen I feel you and I surely have been pre-
served to accomplish [something] superior to this."[11] She told
Barbara that she would like to give lectures on England when
she returned home. She thought Barbara had moved intellectu-
ally ahead of her, but she realized that she had gained different
experiences. For some reason the two did not meet in Chicago,
and, although they continued to write to each other, they apparently never did meet again.

In June 1888, Mattie decided it was possible for her to
return to Utah. Over three years had passed since she left, and
the $200 bond for her arrest for refusing to act as a witness for
the federal agents had expired. She was eager to resume her

practice and, of course, to be again with Angus. She had spent such a long time away from him, and she reasoned she had been away long enough that the marshals would no longer be pursuing her. She returned home to her stepfather's house later that month.

Before her exile abroad, Mattie had had the opportunity to visit New York and Boston to observe the nursing schools in those cities and to purchase textbooks. Her ambition at the time was to start a nursing school in Salt Lake. Of course this plan was disrupted by her exile, but she took advantage of her time in Europe to look into such organizations there as well.

Now back in Salt Lake, she was able, in January 1889, to establish the school, the first nurses training school in Utah. Tuition for a three-month session was twenty-five dollars, and twelve students completed the first session. In addition to giving courses in general nursing and obstetrics in the new school, she reestablished her private practice.

After being away for almost two years, she had looked forward to coming home with great anticipation. In this she was disappointed. She wrote to Barbara a couple of months after her return: "I am busy with my practice, but I have no office or home yet. My anticipations of happy associations with loved ones after my long exile were altogether overdrawn . . . and I find myself enduring one of the veriest practical proxy of lives."[12]

As before, her relationship with Angus was difficult. Shortly after her return, she wrote him: "I imagine I caught a glimpse of you at the theatre last eve—behind the curtains you know and what fair siren had you there with you? Of course you will tell me. Jealous I *am*. Have I cause to be, or was it all vile imagination on my part?"[13] Her jealousy didn't interfere with their intimacy, however, and she soon was pregnant again. Unfortunately, this time she lost her baby when a runaway horse tipped over the carriage she was driving—a little boy she had planned to name Peter after her father.

Since her marriage Mattie had apparently expected to be the one true love of her husband's life. This expectation allowed her to accept Angus's subsequent marriages to Maria Bennion and Johanna Danielson as obligations of his role in the Church hierarchy. But her expectations were repeatedly frustrated. She wrote him in 1889: "How do you think I feel when I meet you driving another plural wife about in a glittering carriage in broad daylight? I am entirely out of money, borrowing to pay some old standing debts. I want our affairs speedily and absolutely adjusted—after all my sacrifice and loss you treat me like a dog—and parade others before my eyes—I will not stand it."[14]

Salt Lake City at this time was one of the dirtiest cities in the West. Although Brigham Young had had a good sense for city planning, creating attractive public buildings and 132-foot-wide boulevards, wide enough to turn a team and wagon around—an amenity of the city still today—the city had swelled in population very quickly, more than doubling from 1880 (20,800) to 1890 (44,800). This stretched its ability to properly absorb the growth, creating a constant mess of building activities and street excavations. Not until the 1890s did the city begin to pave the streets and bury sewer and water lines. The city had installed a settling tank in City Creek Canyon and water mains in 1884, but generally the pipes served only municipal fire hydrants. After a heavy mountain thunderstorm or a warm sun on winter snow, the streets were thick with mud and the droppings left by carriage horses and the mule-drawn streetcars. Typhoid spread easily in the urban area where most of the population drew water from open ditches and wells, the wells often situated too close to privies. The public fountains each had a single tin cup that everyone used. Tuberculosis was rampant in the crowded miners' quarters.

Perhaps the city's worst problem was air pollution. The air was full of toxins spewed from the smelters processing ore in the canyons, and the effects could be seen on the damaged foliage in the parks and residence gardens. Wind and rain blew particulates onto cropland. Additionally a general ignorance of the importance of sanitation and a resistance to the need for quarantine fed the epidemics that coursed through the city, as through many cities of the West.

Utah had no state public health department, and hence no organization officially in charge of dealing with public health issues. This was the environmental situation that Mattie planned to address through public lectures. However, implementation of these plans would have to wait. She had barely reestablished her practice—and barely recovered from her miscarriage—when she again became pregnant. Once more it would be necessary to put her profession on hold and flee Salt Lake City to protect her husband and allow him to carry out his Church responsibilities.

In her manuscript about her mother, Elizabeth Rachel relates an incident at this time that reveals the playfulness of her mother's character. Mattie, extremely pregnant, wanted to see the play, *Josephine,* in the Salt Lake Theatre. She disguised herself as an old woman and had two friends, who masqueraded as men, accompany her. Before the performance was over, the two friends wearing men's clothes were spotted and began to be heckled. As the attention of the audience focused on "Josephine's" death scene, the "old lady" and her two escorts hurried out of the theater before the spectators came out. Mattie got in her buggy, and, in case she was followed, drove around the city until she finally stopped at the place she was staying, the home of John Henry Smith on West Temple. Two nights later, her son James was born.[15]

Among his many duties as stake president, Angus was required to preside as judge of the stake court, which determined both civil and religious cases throughout Salt Lake County, and to conduct the services every Sunday in the tabernacle. He was responsible for the administration of the stake and its many wards, and he was also responsible for six wives and a great number of children. Hence Angus didn't have much money with which to help Mattie. He did what he could, but she was largely on her own to earn her living as a physician. But if he were locked up in jail on another polygamy charge, he'd not be able to provide support to any of them, so it was up to Mattie to take on the consequences of the situation. Maria Bennion, from her hideout in Logan, was nevertheless presenting Angus—and the LDS Church—with a couple of babies at this time: Ira Bennion Cannon, born in February 1889, and Eleanor Bennion Cannon, born January 1891. Mattie and Angus's son, James Hughes Cannon, was born in May 1890, and Mattie immediately left Utah with her two children—this time for San Francisco, once again to live under the name of "Munn."

Mattie's life was not turning out the way she'd dreamed. She again felt the despair of homelessness that had followed her since her marriage and motherhood. "Oh for a home," she wrote Angus from San Francisco, "for a husband of my own because he is my own. A father for my children whom they know by association. And all the little auxiliaries that make life worth living. Will they ever be enjoyed by this storm-tossed exile? Or must life thus drift on and one more victim swell the ranks of the great unsatisfied?"[16]

And to Barbara she wrote with a sense of resigned disappointment:

It's nearly seven years since I launched forth on the great sea of matrimony, and I feel I have not learned the a b c's of the great volume. Have scarcely culled from my sentimental nature those romantic dreams—the sooner they are rooted out and supplanted by the practical facts and conditions of the mundane, the sooner we will attain those tranquil shallows of contentment, far removed from those surging billows of life's ocean that causes us to "sound the heights and depths of human emotions."[17]

For the next decade, there would be no tranquil shallows. When she returned from her second exile, much had happened in Utah that would affect her life and the lives of her fellow Saints.

CHAPTER 8

At the dedication of the Manti Temple in 1888, President Wilford Woodruff announced to the faithful that "we are not going to stop the practice of plural marriage until the Coming of the Son of Man."[1] Two years later, by divine revelation, God countermanded Woodruff's statement. God informed the president that polygamy was no longer to be practiced, and that no further polygamous marriages were to be performed.

The passage of the crushing Edmunds Act in 1882 had caused a surge in the number of polygamous marriages, performed, perhaps, out of anger at the government. In fact, however, by the time of Woodruff's revelation, only some 10 percent of Mormon marriages were polygamous. While the Saints accepted polygamy in theory, few actually carried out the practice, despite the urging of Church leaders.[2]

Some of the leaders accepted the revelation as just that: the God-mandated imperative that, even if it meant sacrificing celestial plural marriage, the prophesy dictates that the LDS Church must survive to meet the Second Coming of Christ. And when He comes, it is the Church that will be called to spread the Kingdom of God on earth. These followers believed in the continuing revelation of *living* prophets, and as Church president, Woodruff was considered a prophet. This belief was essential for these Saints to accept the revelation. Others, many of whom had fought and suffered for the "principle," were convinced that Woodruff had fabricated the "revelation" as a tactical maneuver to save the Church. At the time Congress was debating the Cullom-Strubble Bill, an even stricter bill than the 1887 Edmunds-Tucker Act, the intent of which was to destroy the Church politically by disenfranchising all Church members, polygamous or not. Indeed, some of the General Authorities as well as others were either currently in jail or in danger of being arrested or rearrested. The government receiver was taking possession of Church property, which meant not only material loss, but also economic disaster in that the authorities could no longer borrow against Church assets. It would seem quite reasonable for God to step in with a revelation. The revelation was God's law and hence Church law.

A "Manifesto" against further plural marriages was immediately proclaimed. Woodruff stated in the Manifesto: "I now publicly declare that my advice to the Latter-day Saints is to refrain from contracting any marriage forbidden by the law of the land."[3] The Manifesto was presented to the congregation at the October conference in the Salt Lake tabernacle. The sustaining vote was unanimous—among those who voted. At least half the people didn't vote at all.[4]

The Manifesto, however, left questions: Why did President Woodruff merely declare his "advice" to the Saints? And why, when most revelations were introduced by "Thus saith the Lord," was this revelation introduced with "To whom it may concern"? And what about the status of existing marriages and families? What about performing plural marriages outside the United States, principally in Mexico or Canada? Or maybe even offshore? Did the revelation mean that God had simply changed His mind about the "celestial" aspects of plural marriage? What were the implications for eternity? Did the revelation mean that plural marriage was no longer essential for the highest degree of exaltation? Although plural marriages had been illegal in federal territories since the original Morrill Act in 1862, and even earlier in the state of Illinois, such marriages had had religious approval and encouragement up until now, and plural wives from these marriages were sealed to their husbands by covenant in the House of God. Now the official Church position was that men could and should take care of their former plural wives, but what about cohabitation? The Manifesto didn't address cohabitation. One wonders if either the federal government or the General Authorities actually believed that a man was no longer going to sleep with a woman who, prior to 1890, was sealed to him for eternity, and in most cases was the mother of his Church-blessed children.

Many in the Church, including some of the Apostles, were skeptical that the Manifesto was indeed a revelation and not simply political expediency. Brigham Young Jr. railed that "rulers in this nation will have a heavy bill to settle when they reach the spirit world."[5] But President Woodruff was adamant about the sacred source of the revelation: "I should have let all the temples go out of our hands; I should have gone to prison myself, and let every other man go there, had not the God of Heaven commanded me to do what I did do."[6]

There can be little doubt that some, especially some of the women, may have breathed a sigh of relief after the meeting at the tabernacle conference. For many of them the Manifesto released them from a life of fear and hiding. Some women had been living underground for almost ten years, dragging children from one place to another, never able to settle in their own homes without fear of being roused in the night by a federal agent. Others had been imprisoned for refusing to answer personally invasive questions about their sexual relations. The raids had caused tremendous economic upheavals for individual Mormons as well as for the Church as an organization. While the men were incarcerated, businesses failed and farms went untended and wives and children lived in poverty. The children often were forbidden to play with their friends because it was feared they might say something that would cause a mother or father to be caught. Everyone was suspicious of "skunks"—Mormons who turned their neighbors in so they could collect the bounty; one didn't know whom to trust. With the approval of the Manifesto, finally something had been done, even if it might cause great adversity to some. If a plural family was a loving one, there would be little change; the husband would care for and support his wives. But the Manifesto released women for whom there had been no love, where their relationship in the family had been resented and their children rejected. Of course several cases of nonsupport came before the Church's High Council, and occasionally a first wife who had put up with polygamy against her will was able to force her husband's plural wives out of her home. Whereas during the persecutions of the 1880s, the people had supported each other against the government as the common enemy, after the Manifesto there began to be a stigma attached to polygamous families.[7]

Passage of the Manifesto relieved government pressure on the Saints. Angus, as well as other polygamous husbands, was no longer hounded by the law, and he could return openly to his work. Judge Charles Zane, who had been exceedingly harsh, in effect incarcerating anyone who was up for trial, became far more lenient with those charged with polygamy before his court. Although some anti-Mormons were angered by this leniency, Judge Zane was known to excuse defendants who swore they believed in and would follow the Manifesto. And because the prosecutions diminished, most of the polygamists followed the lead of the Church authorities and surreptitiously continued to live in connubial relations with their wives. The government officials tended to ignore them; it seemed the best way to deal with such infringements was to simply wait until the relationships naturally died out.

In an October 1891 meeting with the Master of Chancery, President Woodruff and Counselors George Q. Cannon and Joseph F. Smith, seeking the return of the Church's escheated properties, testified that no new plural marriages had been performed, even in Mexico, and that there was no further cohabitation. Some of the LDS Church members were shocked at this testimony, suspicious that the statements of their leaders were not true. In January 1893, Republican president Benjamin Harrison issued an amnesty to all who were in compliance with the law since passage of the Manifesto, and a year later, President Grover Cleveland issued an amnesty to all the polygamous men. The amnesty returned the escheated Church properties, and also returned the franchise to the polygamous men, although not to the women.[8] The amnesty was based on the government's agreement with the Church authorities that polygamy had ended and that cohabitation with plural wives was no longer permitted. It soon became evident, however, that the General Authorities had no intention of abiding by their agreement, and their duplicity caused dissention within the Quorum of the Twelve, and generally among the lay members.[9]

For Mattie the Manifesto meant she was able once again to establish her practice without fear of either incriminating Angus or of being called to testify against her husband or her patients. She set up a home-office on the corner of South Temple and First West.[10] She was of course extremely busy with two young children, but if there were times when there was not enough money to hire a house girl to cover her during office hours—which were afternoons from only 2:00 until 4:00, although there were always emergencies—she could take the children to her mother.

Most important to the Saints, the issuance of the Manifesto and the stated commitment of Church authorities to enforce it at long last allowed Congress to consider the enabling legislation that would permit the Utah Territory to become a state. And with the advent of statehood, a new career would open for Mattie, one that would ultimately lead her to the fulfillment of her ambitions.

CHAPTER 9

The women's rights movement in Utah was still a fledgling in 1870 when the territorial legislature enfranchised the women of Utah. With a stroke the second half of the population had the vote. Outside of a dedicated core of activist women, Utah's pioneer women were not immediately involved in this action, most of them busy with their children and domestic duties and, if their husbands were away on missions, caring for family businesses or farms. In February, 1870 only twenty-five Utah women voted; six months later 2,000 women voted. It was not long, however, until in some counties more women than men voted.[1] The enfranchisement action was largely the instrument of men, who brought it about for opposing reasons. Antipolygamists and government officials believed that the franchise would give Mormon women the opportunity to vote themselves out of polygamy; the patriarchal Church members reasoned correctly that the women would defend polygamy for religious reasons, and the women's vote would strengthen LDS hegemony throughout the territory. But as antipolygamist actions became more and more aggressive, the women became more active in their self-defense.

Originally started in Nauvoo by Joseph Smith, the women's Relief Societies, after a hiatus of many years, were reorganized in the late 1860s by Brigham Young's wife, Eliza Snow. These societies brought women together in cooperative ventures and, it would soon turn out, provided a venue in which they could discuss their concerns and organize their protests. Further, with the establishment of the *Woman's Exponent* in 1872—where Mattie worked as a typesetter and where, as a young girl, she became aware of women's issues nationally and internationally—the women found a medium that would bring them information from beyond their isolated settlements and would give them a voice. In the pages of the *Exponent*, they could broadcast to the world the evidence of their education and cultural sophistication and show that they were not the degraded slaves of polygamist masters that the popular image would have. The *Exponent* defended polygamy and argued for women's rights, one of which being the right to enter a plural marriage if one so chooses. It also brought news of the national woman suffrage leaders' activities. When Emmeline Wells—a plural wife herself and one of the women who had encouraged Mattie to attend medical school—took over as editor in 1877, the masthead of the magazine read: "The Rights of Women of Zion and the Rights of Women of All Nations."

In 1870 the Collum Bill, which would have strengthened the 1862 Morrill antipolygamy act, was being debated in Congress. The Relief Societies organized a mass protest and thousands of women came together in the Salt Lake tabernacle in a "great indignation meeting," at which time they sent a resolution to Congress claiming that polygamy was their religious right, and that it was the safeguard of female virtue and protection against the sin of prostitution. They protested against the popular image of the Mormon woman as a slave and pointed out that she was free to divorce at any time with rights of support. Estimates are that perhaps 75 percent of all Mormon women did not live in polygamous marriages at that time. However they defended the practice as a religious principle, and they bonded with their sisters in mutual defense against the stereotype of the degraded Mormon woman. And even those women who were lonely and unhappy in their plural marriages—Emmeline Wells, herself, was such a woman—vehemently defended the practice.[2]

A common enemy gives people a group identity, and in 1878 the Mormon women rose in a mass protest against the recently formed Utah Anti-Polygamy Society that was urging the repeal of women's suffrage in the territory. The Mormon women argued their constitutional right to freedom in the exercise of their religion. The Anti-Polygamy Society began with some two hundred non-Mormon women with the national support of writer Harriet Beecher Stowe, temperance crusader Frances Willard, and First Lady Lucy Hayes. They published the *Anti-Polygamy Standard,* which waged a vicious war against the polygamists and was ultimately instrumental in achieving their goal with the disenfranchisement of all Utah women through the passage of the Edmunds-Tucker Act of 1887.

Having lost the franchise, in 1889 the Mormon women formed their own Utah Woman's Suffrage Association, allied with Susan B. Anthony's National Woman Suffrage Association. Anthony did not approve of polygamy, and in a later communication, she stated that she "abhorred" the practice. However she differentiated between endorsing a movement and endorsing Mormon women.[3] Many of the non-Mormon members of the national association, however, were uneasy about the Utah women's membership because of their defense of polygamy. The Utah women's alliance with the national group further strained relationships between Anthony's National Woman Suffrage Association and the rival American Woman Suffrage Association.

Mattie had no opportunity to actively participate in the new organization's activities because of her San Francisco exile. However, on her return she became a leader in the Utah Woman's Suffrage Association, giving talks to groups throughout Utah and participating in suffrage conferences in the East along with

Susan B. Anthony and Elizabeth Cady Stanton. At the 1893 Columbia Exposition in Chicago, Mattie was a featured speaker at the Woman's Congress. She traveled to Chicago with a group of Utah women leaders. Always tight for funds, she nevertheless telegraphed home for money and bought herself an elegant outfit in the latest fashion for the occasion. According to her daughter's manuscript, Mattie was embarrassed to be seen as another dowdy Utah woman—like those who accompanied her. In her fashionable green outfit—hat, gloves to match—she not only made a splash at the congress with her professional degree and her elocution, but also with her elegance. Describing the strength and character of Utah women, she went far to dispel the caricature of the wretched polygamous slave.[4]

The Utah women took advantage of the fair to distribute a pamphlet boasting of the accomplishments of the primarily female-run Deseret Hospital: "Over four hundred operations, including some of the major operations, have been attended with success. . . . About thirty [nurses] have received certificates and gone to distant parts of the country to fulfill important positions."[5]

Mattie went on from Chicago to appear before a congressional committee in Washington, D.C., to give a status report on the women's suffrage work in Utah. The *Chicago Record* noted that "Mrs. Dr. Martha Hughes Cannon . . . is considered one of the brightest exponents of the women's cause in the United States."[6]

Between the approval of the Manifesto in 1890, which allowed the government to back off from the prosecutions, and the adoption of the state constitution in 1895, which would permit elections for the new state to take place, several events occurred that became politically important for the successful move toward statehood.

By 1892 the national political parties, the Republicans and Democrats, replaced the old Utah parties: the Liberal Party of the Gentiles, and the People's Party, or party of the Saints. This resulted in the coming together of Gentiles and Mormons in each of the parties. Among the Mormons there were reasons of national economic policy for some to favor the Republicans, but many of the Saints were angry with that party because, with only one exception, all the territorial agents and prosecutors sent to harass the Mormons between 1870 and 1890 were Republican appointees. The Church authorities urged members to try to divide themselves as equally as possible between the two national parties so they would not be charged with trying to take political advantage of the situation. Angus moved to the Republicans, Mattie to the Democrats.

The women of the Utah Woman's Suffrage Association were becoming more and more vociferous in their demands that the vote be reinstated. In 1894 Mattie gave a speech that went far beyond the issue of suffrage to the issue of gender equality:

One of the principal reasons why women should vote is that all men and women are created free and equal. No privileged class either of sex, wealth, or descent should be allowed to arise or exist. All persons should have the legal right to be the equal of every other.[7]

Such talk won't be heard again until the debates on the Equal Rights Amendment in the 1970s. However, unlike events of the 1970s, in the discussions surrounding suffrage in 1894–95, most, but not all, the Church leaders favored the women's franchise.

In 1894 Congress passed the Enabling Act, which authorized a constitutional convention to be held the next year, and the women set about lobbying the leaders of the two political parties. In September the Republicans held their convention in Provo, and their platform stated: "We favor the granting of equal suffrage to women." A few days later the Democrats met in Salt Lake City. Their platform also addressed the women: "The Democrats of Utah are unequivocally in favor of woman suffrage."[8] The suffragists had done their lobbying well, but despite the platform statements, the issue was far from resolved. Suffrage associations were organized in most of Utah's counties, and when the counties held their delegate conventions, Dr. Ellen Ferguson, president of the Salt Lake County Suffrage Association, also a physician, sent the members out to talk to the county delegates to be sure they were on board.

The arguments that were being raised against the women, and which were raised nationwide as individual states considered the vote for women, were commonplace among antisuffragists: Women were too "pure" for politics; women would just vote however their husbands or their religious leaders told them to; women were too impulsive, too sympathetic, too delicate to bear the stress; and so on. These were easily dismissed in a world of hardy independent pioneer women, especially women who had already had the vote and then had it taken away from them.

A major problem was developing, however: Many of the delegates, regardless of whether they favored the women's vote, feared that inclusion of the franchise in the state constitution would hold up its passage and hence jeopardize congressional approval of statehood. Further, since the Edmunds-Tucker Act had disenfranchised all Utah women, the Mormon electorate had become much smaller, allowing the Gentiles to begin capturing local elections. It was clear that the opposition worried that the LDS authorities would control the women's vote if the franchise were included. Many non-Mormon women, contrary to their own interests, opposed the franchise for fear of consolidating Mormon hegemony—the potential votes of some thirty thousand women were at stake, and four-fifths of those women were Mormons.

There was a movement to consider the franchise provision separately, either as a separate resolution during the convention or after statehood as a proposition to be submitted to the voters. Susan B. Anthony warned the women not to let this happen. She had plenty of experience in the difficulties of trying to get the vote through in a separate action.

Some of the Church authorities were in favor of the women's vote and some were not. One of the women's staunchest advocates was Bishop Orson Whitney, who argued for the franchise because, "It is a measure of progress, a step in the march of human liberty, and will sweep from its path all opposition that lifts its puny arm and voice against it. I feel this in every fiber of my being."[9]

That puny arm belonged to B. H. Roberts, a lawyer and the Church historian, who spoke eloquently against including the franchise, worried that women would spoil politics and politics would spoil women. The arguments went back and forth for days during the convention. Mattie's brother-in-law, George Q., was opposed to the women, although he had been in favor of the 1870 franchise. Protagonists raised a subject touchy in the American psyche ever since the Revolution: It is unfair to expect women property owners to pay taxes without ballot representation. And the ultraconservative Brigham Young Jr., to the surprise of many, also supported the franchise. Arguing with B. H. Roberts, Young reasoned that since the Manifesto had taken away the women's husbands, the least society could do was to grant them the vote.

The Church didn't dare take an official stand; in addition to being divided among themselves on the issue, its leaders feared being accused of political interference by the Gentiles. The women couldn't vote in their own interests for the constitution because they were still living under the terms of the Edmunds-Tucker Act, which had disenfranchised them. But

Mattie and her suffragist sisters were the wives and daughters of prominent Churchmen and wouldn't hesitate to use their influence where possible. The work the women had done to get the promise of suffrage into the platforms paid off. Some who were actually against putting suffrage in the constitution, including the editor of the *Salt Lake Tribune,* nevertheless felt they had to stand by the people who had voted in the parties on the basis of the platforms.

Supporters of both sides of the issue unleashed a war of petitions, and those for immediately including the women's franchise in the constitution gathered the most signatures. So, after bringing to a close almost two weeks of argument that endlessly repeated the same points, the question was called: By the all-male vote, the women won.

And they won easily. About 20 percent of the men voted against adoption of the constitution, but women's suffrage was a reality for the new state, and Susan B. Anthony and the Reverend Anna Shaw came to Salt Lake to celebrate the words so hard won:

> *Article IV, Section 1: The rights of citizens of the State of Utah to vote and hold office shall not be denied or abridged on account of sex. Both male and female citizens of this state shall enjoy equally all civil, political, and religious rights and privileges.*

President Cleveland signed the constitution in January 1896, and Utah, after six previous attempts, finally achieved statehood. It also became the third state, after Colorado and Wyoming, to grant women the vote. Idaho women would gain the franchise the next year, but it would be another quarter century before women in all the states could vote.

CHAPTER 10

I f the Church leaders were hesitant to be seen as attempting control of the political parties, they were not hesitant in attempting control of their own people. In 1895 one of the Quorum of the Twelve, Apostle Moses Thatcher, accepted the Democratic nomination for state senator. Thatcher was disciplined for not having sought prior approval from the Church authorities. He was defeated in the election, but the following year the Church issued a rule, a "political manifesto," that required all Church members seeking a political position to secure the agreement of the First Presidency that the position wouldn't interfere with their Church responsibilities. Thatcher refused to sign this rule and found himself dropped from the Quorum of the Twelve.[1]

Many of the leading Mormon women, including Mattie and two of her colleagues in medicine, Dr. Ellen Ferguson and Dr. Romania Pratt Penrose, became active in the Democratic Party. *Woman's Exponent* editor, Emmeline Wells, however, became a Republican. In the buildup of expectations for the November 1896 election, national issues were an important distinction between the two state parties. Republican presidential candidate William McKinley favored high tariffs and the maintenance of the gold standard to address the currency crisis that resulted from the "Panic of 1893." The 1893 depression was blamed on the Democrats because it was believed that Grover Cleveland's policy of "free trade," that is, lower tariffs, was what caused the

First Utah State Senate, 1896 (Mattie is front row left.)

economic downturn. The price of silver had declined to half, closing many mines; banks folded all over the country. Zion's Bank and the State Bank of Utah, the two major Mormon banks, managed to avoid collapse through the efforts of a young businessman, Heber J. Grant, who was able to get eastern banks to renew local debt.[2] To add to the economic problems, drought damaged the wheat crop on the western plains, and it was the worst sheep year the Saints had yet seen.

And the Church was in debt. The government had returned the escheated property, but it came back at less than it had been worth, and many Church members had stopped paying their 10 percent tithes, feeling that their money would just be grabbed up by the government receiver. Additionally there was the huge cost of the just completed Salt Lake Temple, as well as other projects for which the Church was in debt.

Against the national economic conditions, the Democrat Party's candidate, William Jennings Bryan, advocated "free silver" as a moderate way to solve the monetary crisis at a rate of sixteen ounces of silver to one ounce of gold, hence the election slogan: 16–1, which was bruited about throughout the country. The Republicans worried this would cause inflation; the Democrats and their Progressive Party associates argued that maintaining the gold standard, as well as high tariffs, was hurting the small farmers and laborers. Among the Republicans in the West, however, were the "Silver Republicans." Angus, as well as many Utah Republicans, was "silver." But only on the point of free silver did they agree with Bryan. Utah was a mining state, and many of the mine owners were badly bruised from the plunge in the value of silver. The Silver Republicans could not go along with Bryan on lowering the tariffs, however. The Republican campaign outspent the Democrats nationally by a factor of ten; the party sent speakers, including Theodore Roosevelt, all over the country to denounce Bryan. Mattie stumped for Bryan, undoubtedly to Republican Angus's annoyance.

Angus felt the Mormon Democrat women were spending too much time at politics, and as stake president he suggested to the women who held positions in his stake that they should either resign their jobs or cease their political activities. Angus, as well as several members of the hierarchy, was concerned that the prominence of the Mormon women in the Democratic Party would cause yet more trouble with the Gentiles.[3] According to a diary entry of Abraham Cannon, a son of George Q., the Gentiles feared the Church intended to use women to accomplish political ends the Church was seeking.[4]

Although Angus claimed to be concerned about the impression the political involvement of Church women would make on the Gentiles, and President Woodruff had advised that the male leaders not get involved in party politics, Angus was apparently not so concerned as he gave out: He decided to accept for himself the Republican nomination for the state senate in the November election. The Republicans supported a slate of five candidates to run at large for the five senate seats from the Salt Lake area. Along with Angus, Emmeline Wells was chosen as one of the contenders. Angus's son George was the state chairman of the Republican Party. George felt that including Emmeline in the slate would be a coup that would bring in women's votes. The Democrats likewise proposed a slate of five for the senate seats, one of whom was Mattie. The editor of the *Salt Lake Tribune*, amused at the idea of the Cannons on opposing tickets, suggested that Mattie and Angus should hold a public debate—needless to say, they declined.[5] Although the Republicans took the nation and elected William McKinley as president, the vote was fairly close: 51 percent to 47 percent. Utah, as did much of the West, went Democratic, voting almost 83 percent for Bryan. At the state level the Democrats took all five

Salt Lake senate seats, making Mattie the nation's first woman state senator.

Many believed that Angus was humiliated at his defeat by Mattie, even though it was not a one-on-one defeat; that is, the entire Democratic slate defeated the Republicans. However any five of the ten candidates could have won. Both Angus and Mattie denied any conflict between them, although the newspapers had great fun with the situation. No Republican women were elected. In addition to Mattie's senate win, two non-Mormon women Democrats, Eurithe LaBarthe and Sarah Anderson, were elected to the lower house, and eleven women were elected throughout the state to county offices.

A later Republican evaluation of the election results found that the women's vote was determinate. But they also realized that a far greater percentage of Mormon women had voted than did Gentile women, and far more Mormon women voted Democratic. Now that the suffrage clause in the constitution was in effect, the women could claim again their previously lost voting rights. The election of 1896 would be the only significant moment of power for the women of Utah and the only moment of power for the Utah Democratic Party for many years.[6]

Mattie's election to the senate gave her the position she had been preparing for since she was a young girl. Now she would have the chance to make a difference in the public health conditions of her people. This was not her only interest; she would be involved with other issues, but public health was her primary concern.

CHAPTER 11

A year after the territorial legislature granted suffrage to the women of Utah in 1870, the "Matriarch of Mormonism," Eliza Snow, predicted, "Although vested with the right of suffrage, we shall never have occasion to vote for lady legislators or for lady congressmen."[1]

Eliza died in 1887—nine years too soon to see the young girl she had mentored belie her prediction. As soon as Mattie took her seat in the senate chamber in 1896, she set to work developing legislation to improve the public health conditions of the new state. In the first month she had successfully introduced three bills: an Act Providing for Compulsory Education of Deaf, Dumb, and Blind Children; an Act to Protect the Health of Women and Girl Employees; and, undoubtedly the most important to her, an Act Creating a State Board of Health and Defining Its Duties.

The act to protect women and girl employees required that employers provide "chairs, stools, or other contrivances" for women to rest on when not actively serving customers or performing other work. Perhaps Mattie's past female problems made her sensitive to the physiological needs of women who were standing all day. Governor Heber Wells appointed Mattie to the board of directors for the School for the Deaf and Dumb, and in the second legislative session, Mattie successfully introduced a bill for the construction of a hospital at the school. She also sponsored the state's first pure food law, and she beat back a consortium of lobbyists intent on abolishing the State Board of Public Examiners. The Board of Public Examiners certified the qualifications of doctors and midwives, thereby preventing incompetents or "quacks" from practicing medicine. In this she would have the support of the Utah Medical Association that had just been established in 1895. An adjunct to the bill creating a board of health was a bill to establish an agency for the collection of vital statistics.

At the end of the first legislative term, in the spirit of the women's recent victory, Governor Wells appointed several women to the new state's various boards of directors. Another woman joined Mattie on the board for the School for the Deaf and Dumb, and Emma McVicker, a suffrage colleague, was appointed to the Board of Regents of the university. Two women were appointed to the board of the Utah Agriculture College, and women made up the entire board of the Utah Silk Commission—which was fitting, in that the women's Relief Society had developed the sericulture industry.

Although Mattie's bill to establish a State Board of Health had passed, there had been opposition. In her second senate term, Mattie introduced a public health bill that provided for regulations regarding contagious diseases. Her effort was to restrict teachers with contagious diseases such as tuberculosis from teaching in public classrooms. At this time the issue of whether tubercular teachers should be employed in the schools was controversial. Even the medical association was divided as to whether TB was a contagious disease.[2] On this issue Mattie had the assistance of a woman colleague, Alice Merrill Horne, who had been elected to the Utah House of Representatives in the 1898 election. Alice was, like Mattie, the mother of young children, and was concerned about teachers with infectious diseases; she was also a member of the House Committee on Public Health. Both women lobbied their respective colleagues and committees up to the point of the final decision. Alice Horne describes her maneuvering with Mattie to get the bill passed:

> *As the Public Health measure lay before the Senate await-*
> *ing the final vote, Mrs. Cannon and I went about scattering*
> *flowers on the desks of the senators, press, messengers, and*
> *employees of the Upper House. This gave David O. Rideout a*
> *fine opportunity to recite poetry; he quoted from Longfellow:*
> *"The Hand That Scatters Flowers." Soon there was a roll call*
> *in the Senate chamber. The bill passed! Up we went to the*
> *Lower House.*[3]

The two women repeated their distribution of flowers to the legislators who apparently couldn't resist their ploy; the bill passed and Governor Wells promptly signed it.

Alice Horne was an artist, and she was determined to convince the state to establish a state-supported arts institute. Again there was opposition. This time it was Mattie's turn to help Alice with her bill for an art institute as Alice had helped her with the public health bill. Some of the legislators thought that certain public works projects were far more worthy of funding. Alice and Mattie repeated their act with the flowers in both houses, and today the State of Utah owns a magnificent art collection, and the art institute—at the time, the first in the country—continues to be a support for Utah artists.

The new State Board of Health faced much opposition, especially in the rural counties. There had been attempts in the past to address issues of public health among the Saints. Joseph Smith had instituted a Board of Health while in Nauvoo, but the people had no understanding of the causes of the epidemics that would surge through the population. On arriving in Utah, the Saints organized a Council of Health in 1849 that met in the home of Dr. Willard Richards, who, with his doctor brother, Levi, had been friends of the Prophet. The doctors involved in the council were Thomsonians. They made a serious attempt to spread practical information on public health, but again their knowledge and their treatments were ineffectual against such contagions as diphtheria, typhoid, cholera, or tuberculosis. They relied mostly on the "miraculous" lobelia: "We need to know but little about the patient, only to know that they are sick. . . . [Lobelia] will remove obstructions wherever found in the whole system and restore a healthy action wherever needed."[4] The women organized a Female Council of Health in 1851. The council concerned itself with women's health and hygiene, including matters of dress.

Dr. Washington Anderson, a close friend of Brigham Young, but not a member of the Church, was elected president of the first Medical Society of Utah in 1870. Anderson was more progressive than the Thomsonians, and he was instrumental in convincing President Young of the necessity to send both men and women to medical training in the East. The society's focus under Anderson's guidance was to develop diagnoses through keen observation of a patient's symptoms and then proper use of drugs—no longer assuming that lobelia or red pepper was the answer to every affliction. Still, it was too early to understand the causes of disease. The Medical Society later morphed into the formal Utah Medical Association in 1895.

In 1888 Dr. M. H. Hardy advocated establishing a board of health that would disseminate information and warnings of polluted water and foods, especially milk. Hardy, too, made no headway with a public that still viewed doctors with a suspicion that in many cases was justified. It wasn't until the 1880s that bloodletting and purgation with calomel were finally stopped through the influence of younger, better-trained doctors. Given the modern realization of the importance of retaining as much blood and liquids in the body as possible, these early doctors undoubtedly did considerable harm.

Although the legislature passed Mattie's bill, the solons were not forthcoming with sufficient funds to adequately address the many problems inherent in setting up and administering an enforcement process. Thomas Beatty, a doctor who had served as the City of Salt Lake Health Commissioner in the mid-1890s, applied for the job of secretary of the seven-member board. He was appointed to the part-time position at $1,000 per year, the only paid position. Beatty gave up a lucrative private practice because of his concern for the unnecessary deaths that were occurring through the people's ignorance. Like Mattie, Beatty saw public health as his personal mission, and he retained his position as head of the board for almost forty years.

Governor Wells appointed Mattie to the Board of Health, her appointment to extend through December 31, 1903. In February 1898, the new board held its first meeting. The members immediately ran into opposition. The board found itself functioning as a livestock sanitation board as well as being responsible for the people's health, and the first order of business was the problem of diseased cattle being shipped within the state. Inspections were required, but the board lacked funding. Sheep with scabies had to be disinfected; those with glanders had to be killed. The board sent out requirements to cities, towns, and counties to establish local boards of health to carry out the state board's regulations. About a third bothered to reply. Two more letters were sent out; only a few others complied. Shipping of sick animals across state lines was an interstate issue, and the federal Bureau of Animal Industry had an inspector in Ogden and a few other places, but again oversight was inadequate. The board sent out information to the jurisdictions on sanitation requirements and also insisted that the school districts must enforce the law that Mattie and Alice Horne had managed to pass regarding teachers afflicted with tuberculosis. Again there was resistance.[5]

Among the many conditions that needed attention was a lack of vital statistics. Beatty tried diligently to convince doctors to use the International Classification of the Causes of Death, rather than such vague terms as "inflammation of the bowels," or "mountain fever," or just "old age," but many of the rural doctors resented being told they had to conform. Every improperly made out death certificate was returned to the reporting doctor for correction, breeding a sense of personal affront. It was years before accurate statistics could be recorded.[6]

The regulations that are listed in the biennial Reports of the Utah State Board of Health for 1897–98 and 1899–1900 indicate the unsanitary conditions that existed in the new state:

No water closets, cesspools, etc. within 50 feet of any well or spring;

No hog yards or piggeries within 100 feet of any natural watercourse;

No animal dead of natural causes fed to pigs;

No offal fed to pigs less than a month before they are killed.

No human burials without a permit.

Embalmers must be licensed.

Quarantine: anyone suspected of infectious disease must be stopped at the state line, and if found on a public conveyance, must be removed.

Houses must show the quarantine flag with the name of the disease printed on it: two weeks for diphtheria, three weeks for scarlet fever. In case of death, flag must show for seven days after. Children cannot attend school for the same periods.

The problem was education of the recalcitrant and money to enforce the new regulations.

Regardless of intensive lobbying and the quaint ploy with bunches of flowers, Mattie was unable to get a bill passed in the legislature that would have required children not vaccinated against smallpox to be kept out of school in case of an epidemic. *Requiring* vaccination seemed impossible. The smallpox epidemic of 1898–99 closed an entire town in Sanpete County. People evaded the quarantine and concealed the disease. The Board of Health sent vaccines, but an editor at the *Deseret News* spread the erroneous information that the vaccine wasn't safe. Although the *News* is a Church organ, some of the Church leaders did not agree with this editor, and George Q. Cannon wrote an article praising the vaccination effort—to no avail. The disease spread throughout the state. Not all doctors reported their cases, and families hid their sick. Some eleven hundred cases were reported, but the board members believed another thousand were not reported. Apostle Brigham Young Jr., who believed that God alone could heal the contagious diseases and calamities coming upon the people, wrote in the *Deseret News* that vaccination of schoolchildren was an example of "Gentile doctors trying to force Babylon into the people and some of them are willing to disease the blood of our children if they can do so, and they think they are doing God's service."[7] Utah was exceptional in the country in opposing vaccination to such an extent, and the board members feared that their opposition would try to repeal their powers. The board passed a compulsory smallpox vaccination ordinance; the legislature promptly repealed it, offering a diatribe on the board's uselessness and incompetence. In fact over the years Secretary Beatty survived more than one attempt by the opposition to fire him.

Despite such sentiments as Brigham Young Jr. expressed, and for all the problems the new Board of Health members encountered, by the late 1890s much of the early prejudice against the medical profession had disappeared. This was largely due to the efforts of doctors of Mattie's generation, who had received modern training in the East and in some cases in Europe. Especially important were the women doctors, who were able to influence the people through the many nursing and midwife courses they offered on obstetrics and the importance of sanitation. Mandatory certification of midwives from 1893 on brought an end to the horror stories, such as one related by Dr. Ellis Shipp of a midwife who managed to kill eight women in succession by using a dirty pair of scissors to cut the umbilical cords of their babies.[8]

By 1890 the first sewer in Salt Lake City had been installed down Main Street. In 1896 a large gravity sewer that drained most of the populated areas of the city was installed, thereby eliminating most of the privies and hence the flies that were responsible for spreading disease. The installation of water pipes did away with private wells, which were so easily polluted by the privies, and the open water ditches, often contaminated by animal feces. The Board of Health managed to get rid of the tin cups by the public water fountains—a single cup by each fountain, used by everyone.

These municipal improvements helped to lower the rate of infantile diarrhea, the leading cause of infant death from polluted milk, and kept down the spread of typhoid, except for that spread by human carriers. Sometimes a carrier was unaware of the danger he or she posed. A person having recovered from the disease can still retain the bacillus for months, even years. It remains present in urine and feces and can be spread by unclean hands into food and water.[9] A typhoid vaccine that helped to bring the disease under control was developed in 1906.

Diphtheria was the second leading cause of death, especially in childhood, where the death rate was 35 to 40 percent. A diphtheria antitoxin was introduced into the United States in 1895—if people could be convinced to use it. Tuberculosis was not as prevalent in Utah as in some of the other states, perhaps in part because of the high dry desert air, although certainly this did not eliminate the disease, especially among the miners and people moving into Utah from other states and abroad. Robert Koch had identified the bacillus that causes TB in 1882, and he thought he had found a remedy in 1890, but it proved ineffective. It was not until 1943, with the discovery of streptomycin, that tuberculosis began to be brought under control. Cholera, scarlet fever, whooping cough, measles, and yellow fever could only be contained by stringent quarantine requirements and sanitation measures. Vaccines for these diseases would become available in the 1930s.

Throughout the 1890s, after Mattie returned from San Francisco and became involved in politics, and the years that she served in the senate and on the Board of Health, she continued her private practice. Because of the demands of raising her children and her legislative duties, her office was only open on weekdays between 2:00 and 4:00 p.m. Often her patients couldn't pay her, or couldn't pay her immediately, and money was very tight. Her letters to Angus during these years are full of requests for financial help, and they display a growing sense of bitterness that she and her children are not being treated fairly, or equally, with his other children and wives.

For some unknown reason Angus kept letters and notes from Mattie from this period, even though they often express irony and sarcasm and are very angry with him for lack of support. He kept them, despite Mattie's frequent admonishments to him to destroy them.[10]

Feb. 21, 1894. Dear Angus, We are out of everything (eat-able). . . . We did half the washing for lack of soap. A predica-ment, isn't it? Mattie

March 30, 1894. Please send remittance for children. You would feel sorry if you missed the honor of seeing to their temporal welfare, I know (?) Hence the reminder.

May 10, 1894. Please send remittance if you possibly can. Promised our son some needed clothes for his 4th birthday and have utterly failed in collecting anything for my work. Yours, etc. Mattie

Angus, along with his sons, had been investing in mines for some years with varying degrees of financial success. Recently these investments had begun to pay off. Mattie angrily refers to Angus's financial ventures:

July 5, 1894. Dear Angus, Please send remittance. . . . Children must be fed and clothed and I suppose it is quite as difficult for me to collect money as yourself, seeing as I cannot get three thousand dollars at a time from a coal mine. I tell you this: I am carrying just as heavy a burden and threatened with just as much disaster as any son you have. . . . nor do I think they have sacrificed more for you than I have, and yet you bestow on them ten times more sympathy and help . . . And when you have thoroughly calloused me towards you and developed in your sons well-defined forms of boobyism through bolstering every weak joint, it will be the natural sequence of your pres-ent procedure. I feel disgraced to be obliged to ask for butter, but unless you can see a just distribution of the products of your farm are made, I care for none. When some members are sufficiently supplied, and others get one or two pounds per

*month (not more), it is time for a change. I shall accept noth-
ing through the hands of another wife, however conscientious
and all but perfection you may deem her. "Love is blind" and
some men are. I'll quit. Mattie*

Mattie complains of being unable to collect money owed
her by a patient, and needs $3.50 to pay a seamstress for the
children: "May 27, '94. Have been trying hard to collect the sum
for her this a.m. but failed. She calls tonight for it to settle her
rent. Yours, etc."

Mattie apparently still has not got the home she has longed
for, and that she had asked Angus for years earlier from Algonac:

*February 9, '96. Dear Angus, The Building Society wants us
to move out of the house because there are two hundred and
fifty-five dollars due. I told them I would pay them $75 out of
the next legislature money I receive, and see if you would add
something to it if they would allow us to remain.*

*May 16, '96. Pesky rent is due again. You are such a dear good
fellow, I only need to remind you of these little matters.*

Mattie had an operation in June 1896, and asked Angus to
come to the hospital and bring some oil and administer to her.
She went to Idaho to recover and wrote to him in August:

*I shall always feel you have been too indifferent about many
things with us. . . . You are too often influenced to slight others who have an equal claim upon you, and have sacrificed
quite as much, and more! than the favored one.*

The letters go on in this vein. It is clear that the passion she
once felt for Angus has cooled into complaints and anger over

his lack of concern for the children. She knows she is no longer the most important wife. She invites him for dinner:

January 10, 1896. [I]f you would care *to come. I would not for the world interfere with anybody's day, however. We modern polygs are learning our station. Slowly, perhaps, but* learning. *Lovingly, Mattie*

We do not know if at this time Mattie was still convinced of the loftiness of living the "principle" of celestial marriage with Angus. Her letters suggest that their relationship, at least on her part, had disintegrated to a mundane bitterness. Yet a polygamous marriage in some ways had benefited Mattie, if at the same time, it had denied her the marital happiness that she clearly yearned for as expressed in her earlier letters. Polygamy gave her both freedom to pursue her medical career and the opportunity to become a mother, which, she believed, as she wrote her friend Barbara Replogle, "is a woman's greatest glory." Yet she was also disappointed that polygamy had inevitably denied her her desire for a romantic love, and it had denied her children a closeness to their father.

Whatever she personally may have felt about polygamy, Mattie defended the principle in public. When the British Fabian Socialist, Beatrice Webb, traveled to Utah to investigate the Mormons, she was introduced to Mattie. Webb was interested in Mattie as a senator, a suffragist, and a doctor, but, knowing that Mattie was a plural wife, she was especially curious about Mattie's views on polygamy. Mattie explained to Webb that the Church believed in polygamy for spiritual reasons, that each Saint taking as many wives as he could afford to support allowed the incarnations of spirits seeking birth. Mattie then went on to say that although this was the Church's view, she would be content to let polygamy be judged on practical grounds, "for a woman to select a really good man as father to her children instead of putting up with any miserable fellow who might be left over by other women. Moreover, a woman might be satisfied with one or two children, and seldom needed more in a husband than a kind protector; her children satisfied her instincts." This female practical independence toward marriage may or may not be what Mattie was feeling at the time. She makes no mention of love or jealousy or any other human emotions. It is unlikely that polygamy would simply come down to "scientific breeding" in Mattie's view, although this is the impression she left with Webb. Ten years before, she had written, "I grow heartily sick and disgusted with it—polygamy."[11] On the other hand, Webb was extremely patronizing in her attitude toward Mattie, writing of her as "our frank little senator," and doubting her wisdom as a senator and her skill as a doctor, without evidence to make such a judgment. Mattie may have just been "putting her on."[12]

One of the arguments opponents used against women's suffrage was that women would simply vote as their husbands told them to. This may or may not have been true, but certainly in Mattie's case it was not. During her time in the senate, Mattie had occasion to thoroughly annoy Angus. One incident concerned the case of Moses Thatcher. The Church leaders were opposed to Thatcher's bid for the Democratic nomination for U.S. senator in 1897. Thatcher had not asked the Church leaders for permission to run and had refused to sign the "political manifesto" requiring him to obtain permission from the First Presidency for any political ambitions he might entertain. The leaders felt Thatcher was disregarding their authority and dropped him from the Quorum of the Twelve in November 1896. The Church had suspicions about Thatcher even earlier: In the 1880s he had opposed a proposal to crown President John Taylor as "prophet, priest, and king."[13] Additionally there were disagreements over business dealings and irritation at Thatcher's belief in the separation of church and state. Furthermore Thatcher had had a serious drug problem, and had received treatment the year before. During discussion of Thatcher's bid for the nomination along with that of others, the legislature could not come to an agreement. Several votes were taken, but none were conclusive. It was bad enough, from Angus's point of view, that during the proceedings Mattie switched her vote from another contender to Thatcher against Angus's wishes and the wishes of the hierarchy. But he must have been exceedingly irritated at the publicity when the *Salt Lake Tribune* printed Mattie's picture, captioned "Thatcher's Champion," and reported that

> *Senator Cannon prefaced her vote with an address so eloquent that despite parliamentary decorum and rigid rules against demonstrations, she was cheered and cheered again at its conclusion. . . . There have been eloquent speeches before in the joint session, but none thrilled the audience as did that of Mrs. Cannon.*

One of the representatives complimented Mattie with the pronouncement that she was "the noblest Roman of them all."[14] The year spent at the National School of Oratory was paying off for Mattie. Ultimately Thatcher was not selected, and to avoid excommunication he later signed a statement for the Church acknowledging he was "in error."[15]

Another incident that demonstrated that Mattie was her own woman when it came to Angus's wishes was the case of Frank J. Cannon. Frank was Angus's nephew, the son of George Q. Cannon. Frank had been elected by the state legislature as the Republican candidate to the U.S. Senate in 1896. Along with his colleague, Arthur Brown, the two were the first senators from the new state, although Frank had served in 1894 as the territorial congressional delegate. During their tenure in Washington, however, there had been some question about the morals of both senators. Moreover Frank had voted against the Dingley Tariff Bill to the anger of the Church leaders, who favored high sugar tariffs to protect Utah's sugar industry. Consequently Frank was out of favor with certain Church leaders, especially First Presidency Counselor Joseph F. Smith, who had a personal financial interest in the sugar industry. Nevertheless, when the Republicans considered the next election cycle, Angus supported his nephew. Frank went to Mattie to enlist her help. She refused. Ostensibly she refused because she was still in office as a Democrat, and Frank was a Republican; however she may have had other reservations as well. Frank did not win the nomination; the Church made it clear that anyone who had voted against the Dingley bill would not receive Church support. Late in the balloting, George Q. Cannon, Frank's father, presented himself as a candidate. Mattie didn't vote for George Q. either. The result of all the balloting was that none of the candidates received a sufficient majority, and Utah's U.S. Senate seat remained unfilled. By 1902 Frank had switched parties and was the head of the Democrats. Soon thereafter he renounced the Church and its leaders altogether and was promptly excommunicated. He went on to become the editor of the *Salt Lake Tribune,* and he proceeded to spend the rest of his life attacking the Church hierarchy.

CHAPTER 12

As a result of her suffrage work, her professional achieve-ments, and her work in the Utah State Senate, Mattie had achieved a national prominence. Mattie's daughter Elizabeth Rachel wrote that the *New York World* published a full-length picture over the caption, "First Woman State Senator"— unfortunately, the picture was of the wrong woman.[1] In 1898 Mattie spoke in Washington, D.C., at the fifty-year celebra-tion of the founding of the women's suffrage movement in Seneca Falls, New York. From there she went on to speak on suffrage to the U.S. House Committee on the Judiciary. Mat-tie gave a long and elegant address describing the positive effects of women's franchise in her state. Since having the vote taken away in 1887, Utah women had been voting for only two years. Achieving the vote again had been a struggle, yet as Mattie pointed out to the congressmen:

> *The story of the struggle for woman's suffrage in Utah is the story of all efforts for the advancement and betterment of humanity, and which has been told over and over since the advent of civilization. . . . I can in all sincerity say that there is a strong and cumulative evidence that even those who opposed equal suffrage with the greatest ability and vehemence, would not now vote for the repeal of the measure.*[2]

She was invited to a reception at the White House, and she comments in a letter to Emmeline Wells, editor of the *Woman's Exponent*, that she found President McKinley to be a great man, "notwithstanding he is not a Democrat."[3]

She was successful in her work in the Utah State Senate, losing on only one of the many bills she introduced: an Act Providing for the Teaching in the Public Schools of the Effects of Alcoholic Drinks and Narcotics on the Human System. This bill reflected an interest in narcotics and drug addiction that she would pursue later in her life. Perhaps because of the strong Mormon influence that abjured the use of alcohol and tobacco, the legislature apparently didn't deem the issue significant. In January 1899, a colleague in the legislature nominated Mattie for the U.S. Senate. Conceivably Utah might have sent the first woman to Congress, preceding by seventeen years Montana's Jeannette Rankin, the first woman elected to the U.S. Congress.

On April 17, 1899, Mattie's rising political career came to an end: She gave birth to her third child, Gwendolyn Hughes Cannon. The *Salt Lake Tribune* reported on April 20:

> *Dr. Martha Hughes Cannon is gaining as much notoriety over giving birth to a baby girl as is accorded an Empress or Queen when an heir to the throne is born. The arrival of the little stranger at the Cannon home in Salt Lake has been telegraphed far and wide.*

The *Denver News* contained this telegraphic story:

> *Salt Lake, Utah. April 20. Dr. Martha Hughes Cannon, State Senator of Utah and the only woman who has ever been voted for as a candidate for United States Senator, is living in polygamy. . . . President Angus M. Cannon, her husband, one*

of the most prominent ecclesiastics of the Mormon church, is receiving the congratulations of his friends on the arrival of a daughter.

We cannot know what Mattie's motivations may have been to conceive another child. As a doctor, she was certainly aware of birth control if she would choose to use it. In an 1896 statement to a reporter for the *San Francisco Examiner*, Mattie had made the following comment:

Motherhood is a great thing, a glorious thing, and it ought to be a successful thing. It will be when it is regulated. Some day there will be a law compelling people to have no more than a certain number of children and the mothers of the land can live as they ought to live.[4]

Perhaps Gwendolyn was a love child, a child she truly wanted from Angus—Mattie was certainly a woman moved by passions, as we've read from her letters, although her passion for Angus seemed rather to have dimmed. She must have known that a post-Manifesto illegitimate child would certainly affect her political career, which at that point showed great promise. But given the brouhaha in 1898 over seating B. H. Roberts in the U.S. House, the fact that she was a polygamous wife may have led her to determine that there would be no political advancement for her outside the state of Utah. Then again, perhaps the baby was just an accident—one of those accidents that changes a person's life. Whatever the reasons or lack thereof, this time she was not going again into exile for Angus's benefit. Her letters and notes to Angus during the period of her pregnancy and after are as scrappy as before:

February 23, 1899. Their shoes are gone. I earned Lizzie's jacket myself . . . so I do not worry you with all things necessary to running a home and the support of [your] children by a long shot.

August 22, 1899. Can you let me have $1.25 for washing. Promised it yesterday. We are entirely out of coal.

April 23, 1899. Please order coal and stop by. I wish to speak to you. (This was six days after Gwendolyn's birth. Angus apparently had to be asked to stop by.)

September 13, 1899. Will you let us have a meat order? It is Elizabeth's birthday and I wish some meat for dinner.

In November was the first time the letters mention "Gwennie," who demanded considerable attention:

November 1, 1899. So interesting to have to write it to my husband! . . . Can you state when you can call—I wish a final talk.[5]

The birth of Gwendolyn Cannon caused a storm of public indignation aimed at both Mattie and Angus, but especially at Angus. The *Salt Lake Tribune* commented that Angus was "a disgrace to the Church. The people say he should get maximum punishment; they are angry that the Authorities have broken their pledge."[6]

Angus was arrested on the charge of unlawful cohabitation. The charges were brought by an irate citizen, an engineer named Charles M. Owen. The *Salt Lake Tribune* in a July 9, 1899, article, WIDESPREAD SENSATION CAUSED BY PROCEEDING, quoted Owen as having filed the charges as a matter of principle. The article is accompanied by a caricature of a distraught Angus holding a squalling infant in his arms with the caption: "You are causing your poor old father much trouble." Angus at first pleaded not guilty—which seems ridiculous under the circumstances—but later changed his plea to guilty.

Owen was actually lifting the lid on an issue that was causing considerable anger within the Mormon community. The terms Congress set for Utah statehood had required the agreement by Church officials that there would be no further polygamous marriages and no further polygamous cohabitation. The return of the federally escheated property, as well as the presidential amnesty, was based on that agreement. This was written into the state constitution and into Utah state law. The birth of Gwendolyn was a blatant example of the fact that members of the Church hierarchy were violating their agreement. When asked why he had brought charges, Owen stated to the *Tribune*:

> *It is a straight question of principle. As I understand the situation, Wilford Woodruff, Lorenzo Snow and others of the highest officials of the church declared under oath . . . that the intent of the solemn manifesto of 1890 was that members of the church of which they were the official representatives would refrain from any further practice of polygamy and its kindred offenses. . . . This they have not done. Mr. Cannon, a high official of the Church of Jesus Christ of Latter-day Saints, cannot plead ignorance of that declaration. Mrs. Martha Hughes Cannon, who has the reputation of being an exceedingly bright woman, is in like condition. There is no doubt in my mind, nor in the minds of any right-thinking members of the community that the conditions that predominated up until 1890 are extending throughout the community.*

Owen goes on to say that the Edmunds-Tucker Act was incorporated into the state constitution, and "in a legislature that adopted that code, Martha Cannon sat as a member, and the prosecution of her polygamous husband will be conducted under that code."[7]

The *Tribune* commented:

> That [Salt Lake Stake] President Angus Cannon has been arrested and charged with living with two or more women as wives ought not cause any surprise. The organ of the Church has been most insolent in its denials of any wrongdoing by high church officials for a whole year, and sneeringly challenging anyone who thought there was any such wrongdoing to bring the matter to trial, pointing out that the courts were open, and all the machinery of the courts were in working order.[8]

Angus's brother, Apostle George Q. Cannon, tried to smooth over the public outrage: "Of course, there will be episodic cases of this kind, but no new polygamist marriages are being entered into, and as I said before, time will soon wipe out the institution entirely. As for myself, I have lived within the law and advised others to do the same."[9] As for his knowledge of no new polygamous marriages, George Q., who authorized his own son's 1896 post-Manifesto polygamous marriage, was lying.

The evangelical group, Christian Endeavour, was outraged both at the news of the birth of Gwendolyn as evidence of ongoing polygamy by Church leaders, as well as the 1898 election of polygamist B. H. Roberts to the U.S. House of Representatives. The two events came to be seen together. A few months earlier there had been meetings in several cities to protest seating Roberts, and a leading figure in the protests was Eugene Young, a grandson of Brigham Young. On the maternal side, Young was

Mattie with daughter Gwendolyn, 1899

also the grandson of Fanny Stenhouse, "that heroic woman who dared to throw off the yoke of Mormonism for herself and her entire family, and then to make a splendid fight to save her sisters from a worse than Egyptian bondage." Young stated that "should [Roberts] be seated, his triumph would be hailed throughout Utah as a manifestation of God's power turning the hearts of the nation toward the Mormon people. It would carry gloom to the women of Utah, whose martyrdom has been too grievous already."[10]

The House refused to seat Roberts, and the Board of Trustees of Christian Endeavour, claiming to represent three million Americans, sent a memorial to Congress urging a constitutional amendment making polygamy and polygamous cohabitation a crime, punishable by among other things, disenfranchisement and disqualification for any state or federal office.

Angus paid a fine of $100 for his polygamous transgression, indicative of the importance a Church-influenced judiciary placed on the offense. Mattie retired to a "quiet life, conducting a limited medical practice and superintending the education of her three children," as reported the next year in the *Deseret Evening News*, Harden Bennion, brother of Angus's fifth wife, Maria—an object of Mattie's jealousy—succeeded Mattie in the Utah State Senate.[11]

Mattie continued her work with the Board of Health for the remainder of her term and maintained her medical practice. She also took part in Democratic Party activities, becoming a delegate to the state convention in 1901, although the Utah Democratic Party was largely in eclipse after 1900. The many business and political interests of Church members were dominant, and the Church had become strongly Republican.

In 1901 George Q. Cannon—First Counselor to the President, brother to Angus, ten-year territorial representative to Congress, polygamous father of twenty-one sons and eleven daughters, missionary to Hawaii, one-time editor of the *Deseret News*, private secretary and son-in-law to Brigham Young, a Church leader since the days of Nauvoo—died. He died in Monterey, California, and when his body was returned to Salt Lake, the people crowded to the station to honor him, standing in the rain for hours waiting for the delayed train. George Q. never became President of the Church, although he was next in line to serve after President Lorenzo Snow, who died a few months after him. A firm believer in the sanctity of "the principle," he once stated:

> *It is a fact worthy of note that the shortest lived nations of which we have record have been monogamic. Rome . . . was a monogamic nation and the numerous evils attending that system early laid the foundation for that ruin which eventually overtook her.*[12]

Cannon did his part to ensure the longevity of the Mormon Empire by producing thirty-two children by his five wives. He also professed belief in the God-given sanctity of the 1890 Manifesto, yet his son, Abraham H. Cannon, entered into a post-Manifesto polygamous marriage in 1896—a rule breaking that opened the door to a large, if unknown, number of polygamous marriages both in the United States and in Mexico, secretly approved by the Church authorities over the next several years.[13]

George Q. Cannon was undoubtedly a great leader of the Church and a major player in its development, yet one wonders of his moral rectitude when he allowed the Brigham Young Trust Company property to be used as a "first class" brothel. Brigham Young's son was outraged and resigned from the Trust—temporarily, as it turned out. Apostle Heber Grant, invited to the opening reception, was stunned to find he had been invited to "a regular whore house." The Church continued to lease property for brothels until 1941, when the First Presidency ended fifty years of leasing to such uses.[14]

The passing of President Lorenzo Snow left the Church in the control of Joseph F. Smith as the new president. Smith promptly filled as many General Authority positions as possible with members of his family, and he continued to do so as opportunities became available, thus creating a blood dynasty that could be expected to support his actions for many years.[15] In order to evidence his control, Smith instructed the Apostles to walk through all doorways in order of seniority—as president, we can assume he was first through the door.[16] Once in power Smith continued to indirectly authorize through others a number of polygamous marriages in defiance of the law. At a meeting to sustain Church officers, a member voted against Smith because of his violation of the law; Smith had the man forcibly removed from the Salt Lake tabernacle.[17]

In 1904 Angus was forced to retire from his position as president of the Salt Lake Stake, a position he had held for twenty-eight years. It was a sad time for the seventy-year-old president. The huge stake was divided into four smaller sections, each with its own president. Angus's great-grandson, Donald Cannon, wrote that Angus knew the Church leaders wanted him removed. This time George Q. wasn't there to look out for his brother, and Angus felt useless and depressed, turning to God as his only support. Perhaps as consolation, the General Authorities made him a patriarch, a position that entailed certain activities in the temple, as well as giving funeral orations and patriarchal blessings to whomever wanted or needed one.[18]

For the next several years Mattie and her children moved back and forth between California and Utah. In September 1904, Mattie wrote Angus from the train to California, "I cannot thank our Heavenly Father enough for opening up my way, so this pleasant, happy change could come into our lives."[19] But she soon became quite sick. She took a cottage in Pacific Grove, hoping that living at sea level would help her recovery. This was the start of a series of attacks of illness that took her frequently to California, until she finally moved there permanently near the end of her life. She wrote to Angus that she was sending Elizabeth Rachel back to Utah to attend the university because Stanford would not accept Lizzie's diploma from Latter-Day Saints University (LDSU). She asked Angus to look out for her, to cheer her up at the loss of her mother and sister and brother's presence for a time. She complained of still being ill, again asking Angus for money, and Lizzie, too, wrote her father from Pacific Grove, to tell him how very sick Mattie was.[20]

The next year Mattie was back in Salt Lake, but she was still not well. She told Angus that she felt her heart couldn't take the altitude of Salt Lake, and that if she died, Lizzie and James would take care of Gwennie. In October 1906, Mattie wrote again from California that her doctor had told her that she should spend a year in Pacific Grove. She was uncomfortable, worrying that her Methodist neighbors might discover she was a Mormon, and she was convinced that Methodists hate Mormons. She lashed out at Angus again: "So far as *real* married life is concerned, a la *our* way of doing that, the whole business loses, or has lost its *zest*."[21] Apparently she felt that her marriage wasn't "real." By Christmastime, Lizzie was teaching school in Mexico, in the Mormon settlement of Colonia Juarez, south of El Paso. She wrote Angus from Mexico that Mattie, still in Pacific Grove, was extremely sick and able to sit up only for an hour every day.[22]

During these years, Angus, too, had serious health problems. In 1900 he had a bad accident when a horse he was riding reared and fell on him, crushing his leg. In 1905 he was seriously ill for some weeks after his favored wife, Amanda, died. Two years later, after a thirty-five mile horseback ride, he suffered a stroke, but gradually he fully recovered.

During the years 1902 to 1905, the LDS Church was embroiled in the Reed Smoot hearings in Washington. Reed Smoot, one of the Twelve Apostles and "the Lord's anointed prophet" in the view of the Church hierarchy, was elected to the U.S. Senate in 1902—with controlling political support from the Church—as a Republican. Five days later letters of protest from irate citizens were sent to the Senate and to President Theodore Roosevelt. Initially Smoot was seated, but a year later a bitter three-year battle ensued in the Senate Committee on Privileges and Elections over whether Smoot should retain his seat. Earlier, the U.S. House had refused to seat B. H. Roberts because he was a polygamist. A congressional investigation in 1900 had shown that Roberts, as well as other Church leaders, had betrayed their agreement with the government regarding polygamy. This time with Smoot, the Church was smart enough not to put forward a polygamist. Nevertheless many believed that because the Church still "secretly" allowed polygamy to continue, Smoot could not swear an oath to uphold the Constitution while being an apostle of a church that breaks the law.

In order to reaffirm the 1890 Manifesto, President Joseph F. Smith issued another manifesto against polygamy in April 1904, for the benefit of the Senate investigating committee. The 1904 Manifesto stated:

> *Inasmuch as there are numerous reports in circulation that plural marriages have been entered into contrary to the official declaration of President Woodruff . . . I, Joseph F. Smith, President . . . hereby affirm and declare that no such mar-*

*riages have been solemnized with the sanction, consent, or
knowledge of the Church of Jesus Christ of Latter-day Saints.*

Smith's "affirmation" was a lie. The statement went on
to say that anyone entering into a plural marriage would be
excommunicated.[23]

President Smith was called to Washington to testify in the
Smoot hearings, and he revealed that since 1890, contrary to the
law, he had produced eleven children by his five wives. His testimony shocked not only the Gentiles, but the Mormons as well;
as did the testimony of Apostle Francis Lyman, the next in line
for the presidency; as did that of four other General Authorities, including the "unseated" B. H. Roberts, as well as that of
a number of lesser lights. According to the March 4, 1904, *New
York Times*, other LDS members, including Moses Thatcher, John
Taylor, and Matthias Cowley, were subpoenaed to testify but
they failed to appear. It was later revealed that several of these
had entered into polygamous marriages or performed marriages for others since the Manifesto.

Angus, too, was subpoenaed before the committee. He
agreed to testify only if he would be granted immunity. The
fact of Gwendolyn's birth was, of course, common knowledge.
What wasn't known, at least to the congressional committee,
was that Maria Bennion had given birth to a child in 1891 and
another in 1897. Further, no mention is made in the hearings of
Angus's son, George Mousley Cannon, who married a plural
wife in 1901. Angus confessed to having six wives, all living. He
made the same statement to the committee that he had made
to Judge Zane nineteen years earlier when he had determined
to go to prison rather than abandon his families. He would not
give up his wives, although he said he would not parade them
around in public. Angus's testimony acknowledged his unlawful cohabitation, just as it had in 1885.

In addition to the discussion of polygamy, the committee wanted to know the nature of the oaths taken in the Endowment House and the temples, because it was alleged that these oaths were taken in revenge against the government for past offenses. Smoot had denied any such thing, and Angus refused to disclose the oaths, stating, "God had made it known that the sacred covenants should not be spoken of to the world."[24]

President Joseph F. Smith clearly had no intention of obeying the law. Indeed, when Heber Grant asked Smith in 1891 if he believed the Manifesto was a revelation of God, Smith had answered "no"—he did not believe the Manifesto abolished plural marriage or cohabitation. In the Smoot hearings he arrogantly denied the right of Congress to regulate his private conduct as a polygamist. "It is the law of my state to which I am amenable, and if the officers of the law have not done their duty toward me I cannot blame them. I think they have some respect for me."[25]

After three years of hearings, the committee determined that Smoot should not retain his seat. The majority report declared in bold, THE MANIFESTO IS A DECEPTION.[26] However, with extreme pressure from President Roosevelt—who had suddenly become a supporter of the Mormons after previously strongly disapproving of seating Smoot—the full Senate agreed to seat him. Roosevelt's change of heart came as a result of a deal between the Church and the Republican Party. The constitutional amendment that was proposed by Christian Endeavor and other anti-polygamy groups would have put polygamy and cohabitation once again under federal jurisdiction, as it had been before Utah's statehood. Roosevelt and Republican Party leader Mark Hanna guaranteed they would arrange for the defeat of the proposed amendment in return for Church support of the party.

At the time of the Smoot hearings and as the result of later research, it finally was confirmed to the public that, contrary to the agreements of Church leaders with the government concerning the 1890 Manifesto as being a dictate of God, the Church presidency had been approving polygamous marriages both in the United States and Mexico, and a few in Canada. These illegal authorizations were sanctioned by all three presidents between 1890 and 1904: Woodruff, who in his nineties, purportedly married another plural wife; Lorenzo Snow, who, although living with his last polygamous wife, tried to stop the new marriages, at least in the United States; and Joseph F. Smith, who refused to abide by the law, and stated quite openly to the U.S. Senate Committee members investigating Smoot that polygamy was none of their affair. When the senators asked Smith how he justified breaking the law, Smith replied with a very involved and contradictory argument, stating that he adhered both to the divine revelation commanding polygamy and the divine revelation "suspending" the command.[27]

In 1906, at the birth of President Smith's twelfth post-Manifesto child in Utah, engineer Owen—the same man who had caused Angus to be arrested—filed a complaint against Smith for unlawful cohabitation. Smith was arrested, pleaded guilty, and was fined $300. Such hardship was the "respect" the state judiciary paid to President Smith.[28]

Reed Smoot served in the Senate for thirty years. He was the author of the 1930 Smoot-Hawley Tariff Act, which raised import tariffs on countless imports, causing retaliatory tariffs by other countries. United States trade declined as a result, intensifying the Great Depression. After the economic disaster of the tariff and with the nation in a deepening economic depression, Smoot lost the 1932 election. And for the first time since the 1916 election of Woodrow Wilson, Utah supported a Democrat candidate for president, Franklin Delano Roosevelt.

CHAPTER 13

W e don't know Mattie's reaction to the revelations of the
hypocrisy of Church leaders exposed in the Smoot hearings or to the gossip about illegal marriages bruited about among
the Saints. Mattie herself was guilty of "unlawful cohabitation"
with Angus. But her marriage was sanctified as a celestial part-
nership with the sacramental blessing of the Church, and she
had been sealed to Angus for eternity in the Endowment House.
Her marriage, though technically illegal in government terms,
occurred in a very different social and cultural setting from the
post-Manifesto marriages.

Even before 1890 President Woodruff, still a fervent believer
in "the principle," nevertheless had discouraged further plural
marriages because of the clear intent of the federal government
to destroy the economic viability of the Church. When Woodruff
heard that a plural marriage had been performed in the Endowment House without his knowledge, he had the structure razed.
Yet as Mattie told Angus in an early letter, if her destiny were
not ordained by God, she would have given "the whole plural
system a wide berth." Now she's found that her marriage is no
longer ordained by God—at least not in this mortal world.

As a doctor, principally of women's diseases and obstetrics, Mattie must have been aware of the babies born in post-
Manifesto polygamous relationships, and the suffering some of
these births may have caused the mothers. Aside, perhaps, from
the marriages performed for the benefit of the General Authori-

ties, where the husband had social standing and presumably some money, if we take historian Kenneth Cannon's estimate of 250 post-Manifesto plural marriages, these marriages were clandestine and without any legal or ecclesiastical protection for the wife or the children.[1] Often there wasn't any documentation of the alliance, since the Church was careful not to leave written evidence of its lawbreaking. In his 1911 diatribe against the Mormon leaders, *Under the Prophet in Utah*, Frank J. Cannon, Angus's renegade nephew, calls these unions "polygamy without honor—polygamy *against* an assumed revelation of God instead of by virtue of one." In his book he describes what he calls the "new polygamy":

> *This is the "new polygamy" of Mormonism. The Church leaders dare not acknowledge it for fear of the national consequences. They dare not even secretly issue certificates of plural marriage, lest the record should be betrayed. They protect the polygamist by a conspiracy of falsehood that is almost as shameful as the shame it seeks to cover; and the infection of the duplicity spreads like a plague to corrupt the whole social life of the people. The wife of a new polygamist cannot claim a husband; she has no social status. . . . Her children are taught that they must not use a father's name. . . . They are born in falsehood and bred to the living of a lie."[2]*

As editor of the *Salt Lake Tribune*, Frank Cannon was made aware of many a sorrowful tale of women abandoned by their so-called husbands without any possibility of social redemption or legal or financial rectitude. He notes that young girls were talked into a plural marriage with the argument that it really was still secretly approved by the Church leaders; some of these girls were unaware of the authority of the man who performed the paperless ceremony.

For a woman whose life had conformed—if at times at great emotional cost—to the sacred doctrines of the Church, it is most likely that Mattie would have been extremely disturbed by the hypocrisy shown by the leaders in authorizing further polygamous marriages after their affirming the Manifesto as divine revelation. Indeed she had told Angus years before, "if it were not for daily petitions to God for strength, the Adversary would make me feel it is really a condition of degradation." For some women it appears that plural marriage had indeed become a condition of degradation.

If we can assume that Mattie was disturbed by the duplicity of the Church leaders, this might explain the antipathy toward Mattie evidenced by President Joseph F. Smith in the following incident: Due to a lack of funds, Deseret Hospital, where Mattie had been the resident physician, was forced to close in the early 1890s. Through the generous legacy of an eccentric Mormon dentist, a new LDS hospital, the William H. Groves Hospital, was established in January 1905. The new hospital was opened to great fanfare by President Smith and the Quorum of the Twelve, the Presiding Bishopric, the medical staff, the bishops of the city wards, and sundry guests. The *Deseret News* reported on January 6, that, as at the earlier LDS hospital, "the hospital is to be conducted along the lines of 'Mormon regulations'"—laying on of hands, prayer, ritual administration of sacred oil.[3] The hospital planned to use Relief Society nurses, and Mattie hoped to become a member of the board of the new hospital. However, a revealing entry made on February 4, 1905, in the diary of Emmeline Wells, then head of the Relief Society, suggests that Mattie—perhaps as had Angus the year before when asked to resign his stake presidency—had fallen out of favor with the Smith presidency:

Later Sister Smith and Julina [wives of President Smith] came and wanted to speak to me alone. We went in the other room

*and they told me President Smith wished me or requested me
to tell Mattie Cannon she was not wanted at our meetings [of
the Relief Society] and to ask her to resign. . . . I feel it very
keenly and it seems impossible for me to do. Dr. Allen came
in and spoke to us in our meeting today about nurses for the
new hospital. I am brokenhearted over this affair with Mattie
Cannon. . . . I arose early and went away to the Temple and
mailed my letter on the way."*[4]

This rebuff didn't end Mattie's association with Salt Lake—
she was still an avid Democrat, and the next year found her giving a talk at the Women's Democratic Club on Thomas Jefferson's
love affairs. The gathering was very upbeat about the prospects
of the Democratic Party for the nation. Mattie predicted that "the
spirit of democracy which Jefferson breathed into the Democratic
Party would last forever."[5] Unfortunately for the Salt Lake Democrats, this was precisely the time that the Smith Church had made
its deal in Washington with the Republicans.

After Mattie's moment of political fame in the state senate, as
the *Deseret News* story reported, she began to lead a much qui-
eter life. She continued her medical practice from her office at
Number 11, South First West, and the newspapers report her
presence in many social gatherings, including a select party
at the home of Amelia Young, Brigham Young's favorite wife.
The elderly Amelia was the doyenne of Salt Lake society. Mattie had occasionally accompanied Amelia to the theater, but the
old woman had not actively participated in the social scene for
some time. The party, in Brigham Young's elegant Lion House,
was for a group of sixty, and it says something of Mattie's continued social position that her name was on the guest list.[6]

Mattie's participation as a member of the State Board of
Health allowed her to expand her professional interests. In 1902

Mattie, ca. 1907

she became a member of the psychology section of the Medico-Legal Society of New York.[7] The society was interested in many different aspects of public health and sponsored annual meetings of the American Congress of Tuberculosis. Tuberculosis was a major public health issue worldwide. The bacillus that caused the disease had only recently been discovered, and the congress was focused on international legal means as well as medical and sociological considerations to mitigate the problem. The disease thrived in the cramped, unhealthy tenements of the cities, but it also was a problem in any enclosed space that held large gatherings, such as churches or schools or theaters. And especially for the poor, who had no means to take six months to a year off from their lives to take the sanitarium cure, the disease was usually fatal. Several vice presidents of the congress were selected from the states, and Mattie represented Utah, along with Governor Heber Wells, who was an honorary vice president.

In 1912 Lizzie wrote to Angus from New York and sent her condolences to him at the death of "Aunt Sarah," his first wife. Mattie was again in New York for the Medico-Legal Society meetings, and Lizzie reported that Mattie was in the hospital there with gastritis and an ulcerated sore throat.[8] Mattie recovered her health in time to return to Salt Lake to celebrate Elizabeth Rachel's wedding to Roy Stillman Porter in the Salt Lake Temple. Ann Cannon, Angus's daughter with Sarah, celebrated the wedding with a breakfast for the relatives.

Lizzie's husband, Roy Porter, was a stockman and a farmer. Like his father-in-law, he was involved in public works, building bridges and canals and paving roads. He was also a stockholder in the Utah and Salt Lake Canal Company that was one of Angus's enterprises. He was a devout Church member and a member of the High Priests Quorum. But unlike Republican Angus, Roy was the Democratic chairman of his district. After the wedding Lizzie and her husband moved to Roy's ranch,

"The Oasis," near Brighton, southwest of Salt Lake City. Mattie, in time, would make extended stays at the ranch.

In June 1915 Angus died. He had celebrated his eighty-first birthday just three weeks earlier with as many of his 113 descendants as were able to attend. His obituary recounts the life of a man who was one of the many pioneers who helped to develop the West. Born on the Isle of Man, Angus, like Mattie later, came as a child to America with his Mormon-convert family. His mother died on the voyage across the Atlantic, and his father died not long after arriving in America, leaving six children. Angus first became a farmer, then a stock raiser, a soldier in the Nauvoo Legion, then a printer's apprentice with the *Deseret News*, where he later became the paper's business manager. He spent several years as a missionary and then returned to Utah to work in a pottery business. In the early 1860s he was a member of a committee that went to southern Utah at Brigham Young's behest to establish the town of St. George. The committee elected Angus mayor of the new town, which at that point was a town of tents. In 1876 he became president of the Salt Lake Stake, which had a population of twenty thousand souls for whom he was responsible, both for their civil as well as their spiritual needs. In his later years he became a horse breeder, acquiring his stock from railroad tycoon, senator, and race horse breeder Leland Stanford. He developed a number of mines along the Wasatch Front, and designed a system of irrigation canals throughout the Salt Lake Valley. He installed great pumps at the outlet to Utah Lake that supplied the valley farmland at times of low water.[9] Although without formal education, he educated himself through his own commitment to learning.

Although noting at the birthday party the 113 descendants, Angus's obituary makes no specific mention of his wives and many children, so we can't know if Mattie and her children were present. However, her picture is in a photo of another huge family birthday party for Angus, and since they were living in Salt Lake, we may assume they were present at this one.

In the years after Angus died, Mattie still maintained her office in Salt Lake. She had Gwendolyn with her, and a close association with her Paul brothers and sisters. Mattie's sister, Maude Paul, was a schoolteacher, and her brother, Joshua Paul, was a professor of English and the natural sciences. Joshua was president of the Utah State Agricultural College in Logan and LDS University. Until his retirement in 1928, he was a professor at the University of Utah. Like Mattie, Joshua was a Democrat, and he was nominated twice as the party's candidate for Congress. Gwendolyn was in high school and showed much artistic and musical talent. After her high school graduation, Gwendolyn and Mattie joined James for six months in Los Angeles, where he had settled after attending the LDS Business College in Utah. James had married and was starting the electrical business that over the years would grow into the Cannon Electric Company.

During the Great War there was a scarce number of doctors and nurses on the home front. Those like Mattie, who because of age had not been called overseas, were stretched to deal with the usual maladies that afflicted the population. But suddenly in 1918, near the end of the war, the entire world was attacked by the flu—a flu that killed more people worldwide during the months of its most intense virulence than were killed in the war itself. Many historians conclude that the flu sickness and deaths of the troops on both sides of the conflict precipitated the war's end. All physicians, at home and abroad, were confronted with the disaster. According to her daughter's manuscript, Mattie was called to go overseas, but before she could leave, the war ended. The Mormon Church was also not spared in the pandemic; the flu killed President Joseph F. Smith.

After the war Mattie became involved in fund-raising for war orphans abroad. At the end of the Turkish war of independence in 1922, Atatürk, leader of modern Turkey, pillaged and burned the three-thousand-year-old city of Smyrna, slaughtering thousands of Greeks and Armenians, creating 160,000 homeless refugees. Mattie raised funds for the American Women's Hospitals, founded by a group of women doctors committed to working overseas. With Mattie's help, $500,000 was raised in support of medical relief. American Women's Hospitals took on the responsibility for all orphan and relief work in Greece, paying the salaries for medical personnel and providing medical supplies.[10]

Nineteen-twenty found Mattie and Gwendolyn at the Oasis Ranch, the ranch of Elizabeth Rachel and her late husband Roy Porter.[11] It was a sad time for the family. Lizzie had lost her first baby—a boy. Then in 1919 Roy Porter died, just seven years after his marriage with Lizzie, and a month before his second daughter, Mary Idelia, was born.

Gwendolyn married a young lieutenant, Gerald Churchill Quick of Los Angeles, in 1922. After Gwendolyn's wedding and departure from Utah, Mattie and Lizzie and Lizzie's two daughters left the Oasis Ranch and joined James and Gwendolyn and their families in the Los Angeles area. Gwendolyn was twenty-two when she married, and her husband only a year older. She died when she was twenty-nine, leaving a young husband, a five-year-old son, and Mattie with a broken heart.

CHAPTER 14

After moving permanently to Los Angeles, Mattie apparently did not attempt to establish a private practice. She worked for several years at the Selwyn Emmett Graves Memorial Dispensary, which, in addition to being a clinic for the poor, also served as a teaching facility for students at the University of California, and was part of the UCLA medical program. According to her daughter Lizzie's manuscript, she became interested in narcotics and drug problems, although she apparently did not publish on this subject.[1] She also maintained her contacts with the suffrage movement, which was still alive after passage of the Nineteenth Amendment in 1920. The *Salt Lake Tribune* reports that in February 1927, Mattie attended the thirtieth annual convention of the American Suffrage Association in Washington, D.C.[2]

Whatever Mattie may have felt about the duplicity of the Church leaders regarding continued illegal plural marriages in the period after 1890, her friends and family affirm that she remained a steadfast Mormon. She raised her children in the Church, and both James and Elizabeth Rachel remained in the Church all their lives. Lizzie became a writer, and in 1913 she published a book with her uncle Joshua Paul, the University of Utah professor of natural sciences, on the plants and animals of the Rockies and how they could be useful to humans. Later she produced several romantic semihistorical novels and short stories about Mexico and about Mormon history. In 1941 Lizzie married George McCrimmon in Santa Ana, California.

James studied electrical engineering and became an inventor of electrical equipment. At age nineteen, according to his sister Lizzie, he was managing the Idaho Electric Company at Boise, in charge of a workforce of fifteen. At twenty-one he went to Los Angeles and soon started his own business, later becoming president of the Los Angeles Chamber of Commerce. His Cannon Electric Company supplied special equipment to the movie industry, and produced equipment for fire and police alarms and hospital call systems. During World War II, Cannon Electric supplied a special electrical connector for aircraft, the "Cannon plug." At its busiest time, the company had over 2,200 employees.[3]

Mattie spent her last years in a little house in Los Angeles that James had built for her behind his own house at 4034 Homer Street. When she died, after an operation on July 10, 1932, she left behind James and Elizabeth Rachel and six grandchildren. At Mattie's request, James burned her diaries after her death. Her funeral was in Salt Lake's Tenth Ward Chapel, where she had taught Sunday school many years earlier, and where, in 1878, her friends had held a fund-raiser in the ward hall to send her off to medical school. B. H. Roberts was one of the speakers. Roberts had become Mattie's friend after fighting her over the women's suffrage clause almost forty years earlier, and they had been linked in the polygamy scandal of 1898 and 1899. The other speaker was Mattie's colleague from her days in the senate, Alice Merrill Horne.[4]

For all that Martha Hughes Cannon had publicly accomplished with such determination in her life—her early medical education and practice and later professional interests, her rousing speeches for women's rights across the nation, her concern for the health of the public, and her legislative achievements as the first woman state senator—at her death, she slipped into the memory of only her immediate family.

The stalwart ambition that Martha Hughes Cannon evidenced as a pioneer for women's rights had been rewarded at the time by the leaders of the Church. Indeed it was President Brigham Young who had encouraged Mattie and the sisters of Zion when he called them to study "law or physic" in the 1870s:

> *We believe women are useful, not just to sweep houses, wash dishes, make beds, and raise babies, but that they should stand behind the counter, study law or physic . . . all this to enlarge their usefulness for the benefit of society. . . . In following these things they are but answering the design of their creation."[5]*

As a result of the spirit instilled in the women of Mattie's generation by President Young, we can appreciate her achievement and her belief about the value of women's work, and her belief that work did indeed answer the design of her creation. In an interview with the *San Francisco Examiner* in 1896, Mattie said:

> *Somehow I know that women who stay home all the time have the most unpleasant homes there are. You give me a woman who thinks about something besides cook stoves and wash tubs and baby flannels, and I'll show you, nine times out of ten, a successful mother.[6]*

Today, such a statement might easily have come from a member of the National Organization of Women (NOW). But only in the nineteenth century would such a statement win acclaim in the LDS Church. In 1895 First Presidency Counselor Joseph F. Smith stated in a long and passionate speech to the general conference of the Relief Societies:

Why shall one be admitted to all the avenues of mental and physical progress and the other prohibited and prescribed within certain narrow limits, to her material abridgement and detriment? . . . [S]hall a man be paid higher wages than is paid to a woman for doing no better than she does the very same work? . . . By what process of reasoning can it be shown that a woman standing at the head of a family, with all the responsibility resting upon her to provide for them, should be deprived of the avenues and ways or means that a man in like circumstances may enjoy to provide for them? . . . If the women have equal rights, they must bear equal burdens with men. . . . [T]hey do this already, except that their burdens are made unequal in that they are deprived of the enjoyment of equal rights.[7]

Noble words, indeed, although it might be noted that Smith also commented that God does not reveal his mind to a woman—which fortunately, in Smith's view, didn't interfere with equal rights as a secular matter.[8] At least what Brigham Young and Joseph F. Smith were expressing was a positive attitude in the Church toward women's rights.

But that attitude began to change in the decades after the turn of the century. It was a period when the Mormon Church was leaving behind its image as an isolated cult and attempting to integrate into the greater American society. Mattie's life covered this period of transition, and indeed she was affected by these changes.

It is a curious irony that polygamy, so abhorred in the nineteenth century by the anti-Mormons as suppressive of women's rights, in some ways offered married women greater rights than existed outside Mormondom. The situation that is reflected—perhaps inadvertently—by Joseph F. Smith in his Relief Society speech is that Mormon women who lived in polygamy were for the most part "standing at the head of the family." They were effectively single mothers, as was Mattie, responsible for their own keep and that of their children. As Mattie said to the reporter from the *San Francisco Examiner*—no doubt with some amusement—"If a husband has four wives, she has three weeks of freedom every month."[9]

Mormon women in the mid-nineteenth century were urged by the Church elite to enter plural marriages for the benefit of their life in the heavenly spirit world, but particularly for the present benefit of a struggling pioneer society. The economic situation required women to take charge of their families and their own livelihood. Men were often away on missionary efforts or involved in the duties of building the Mormon society throughout the Utah Territory and adjacent settlements, principally in Arizona, Nevada, and Idaho. Hence many women's rights were not something to be claimed, they were simply *exercised*—not as a conscious "right," but as a matter of daily necessity. Of course women were to be submissive to their men; the society was based on a strict hierarchical order. The men were submissive to their stake and ward leaders, who were submissive to the Twelve, who were submissive to the First Presidency, who took their orders from On High.

While some of the plural marriages were peaceful, that is, the women were capable of sexually sharing their husband and still remaining friends with each other, the "principle" of polygamy was to produce population for the benefit of the whole community, and certainly to benefit the elite of the hierarchy in the here and now. The reward for both the women and the men—but especially the women, since their reward was dependent on the men—was the promise of celestial exaltation.

Polygamy in its nature negated romantic love. Because of this sister-wives were able in some cases to form close bonds of affection and mutual support. Mattie believed in this principle, but not in the manner of older plural wives who counseled their sister Saints—for the sake of their emotional self-protection—not to let feelings of love confuse them in their couplings. The romantic side of Mattie's nature expected more from her marriage with Angus than "a few stolen interviews tinctured with the dread of discovery." But the hard practical facts of polygamy, including its illegality, left her disappointed, jealous, furtive, and often angry. And she was soon to face the transition of the Mormon society away from the principle she believed had been ordained by God, and for which she had sacrificed her desire for a close marital relationship and a father for her children "whom they know by association." And as the principal LDS Church renounced polygamy—however long it took the leaders to accept its demise—the women ceased to have the independence that polygamy had required of them as heads of families and often sole providers for themselves and their children. The priesthood gradually claimed full control of the society. The positive attitudes toward women's rights expressed by Brigham Young and later by Joseph F. Smith began to change to a heightened focus on the family—but a family at which a woman no longer "stood at the head"—and certain women's religious practices and entitlements, as well as women's secular provinces, began to be taken away by the patriarchy.

The Prophet in the early days of the Church had authorized women to administer to the sick through anointing with oil and the laying on of hands. He had even told the women of the Relief Society that these ministrations were "according to revelation . . . and that angels cannot be restrained from being your associates."[10] After the move to Utah, Eliza Snow, speaking to a Relief Society meeting, affirmed the Prophet's statements that all women have the right and duty to administer to their sisters as God had graciously committed to his daughters as well as his sons. And Brigham Young told the women:

If you want the mind and the will of God at such a time, get it; it is just as much your privilege as of any other member of the Church and the Kingdom of God.[11]

In 1888 President Woodruff reiterated the same message: The women were empowered to administer washing and anointing, there was no need to call the brethren.

This extremely important spiritual authority, which permitted the power of God to pass through the hands of the healer to the patient, was gradually taken from the women: The men felt they must control the healing power within the priesthood. In 1914 Joseph F. Smith sent a letter to all bishops and stake presidents instructing them that blessing the sick by women was not an official function of the Relief Society, and that any such blessings were not by ordinance, that is, not officially sanctioned by the Church. Such work was to come under the direction of the bishop.[12] This certainly appears to be counter to the intent of the earlier prophets. In 1943 the Church issued a handbook for Mormon servicemen in the war that counseled: "The Lord has given no set forms in administering to the sick, but care should be taken that it should be done in the name of Jesus Christ and in the authority of the priesthood.[13] By 1946 women were not allowed to administer to the sick at all; a member of the priesthood must always be called to perform the healing.[14]

In 1960 the Church eliminated what financial enterprises the women's Relief Society still controlled and formalized its instruction to women as to their duties as wives and mothers. Since its nineteenth-century organization in Nauvoo and its later reorganization by Eliza Snow, the women's Relief Society, as well as the magazine that was largely associated with the society in its earlier years, the *Woman's Exponent,* had been independent of male control. The women's economic endeavors—sewing cooperatives, grain gleaning and storage, and silk production, as

well as their humanitarian assistance and the fund-raising necessary to acquire the buildings to house the society's projects—
had been the financial responsibility of the women alone. The
women had sent sixteen carloads of their grain to San Francisco
after the 1906 earthquake, and the next year they sent grain to
relieve famine in China. Over two hundred thousand bushels,
sold at $1.20 each, were sent to the U.S. government in 1918 for
the war effort. But this time the bushels were taken by members
of the priesthood and sold without notifying the head of the
Relief Society, Emmeline Wells, until after the fact. The money
from the sale was deposited in a bank until the Presiding Bishopric or the First Presidency decided how it would be used. The
women were told that from then on their production was to be
under priesthood control.[15]

In 1970 the women's fifty-year-old *Relief Society Magazine*,
the successor to the *Exponent,* was canceled. The women were
encouraged to keep up their helpful community services, but
otherwise they were to forget whatever aspirations they might
entertain and go home and take up their wifely duties.

From the late 1950s on, the "Women's Movement" began to
take off in this country, fed by revolutionary publications such as
Simone de Beauvoir's *The Second Sex,* Gloria Steinem's *MS* magazine, Betty Friedan's *The Feminine Mystique* and her subsequent
organization of NOW—the National Organization of Women.[16]
Feminist activism paralleled other activist movements in the society: civil rights activism, initially in the South but soon spreading throughout the country, and student protests, in part over
curricula and free speech, but closely tied to the antiwar movement. Through their own political pressure, the greater society of
women began to gain economic and legal milestones: effective
birth control; the Equal Pay Act of 1963; the 1972 Title IX protec-
tions of equal opportunity in the Educational Amendments Act,
which had been amended to prohibit discrimination on the basis

of sex; the Equal Credit Opportunity Act of 1975; rights of reproductive choice under *Roe v. Wade*; and a decade later a woman,
and then another, on the bench of the U.S. Supreme Court.

Mormon Church leaders perceived these events as threatening the family structure. In 1970 the Church shut down
all semi-independent Church publications, a process they
called "Priesthood Correlation." Ostensibly correlating all
publications—from Sunday school lesson plans to mission
publications—would unify the Mormon message worldwide;
it also was very helpful in controlling the nature and outflow
of information. A new magazine, *Ensign,* replaced all former
periodicals published by Church auxiliaries.

One of the milestones proposed for the advancement of
women's rights was the Equal Rights Amendment to the U.S.
Constitution, introduced first into Congress in 1923 by suffrage
leader Alice Paul. The ERA was a simple statement: "Equality
of Rights under the Law shall not be denied or abridged by the
United States or any State on account of sex." After forty-nine
years of ignoring the proposed amendment, Congress finally
got around to passing it in 1972.

As the amendment moved through the several state legislatures seeking ratification in the 1970s, the conservative leaders of the Mormon Church, along with groups of the Religious
Right, saw the ERA as a call to arms. The Mormon leaders didn't
seem to notice that the wording of the ERA was almost identical
to that of their own Utah State Constitution—"Both male and
female citizens of the State shall enjoy equally all civil, political, and religious rights and privileges." This was the wording
that Mattie and her suffrage sisters, as well as the liberal men of
Mormondom, had fought to secure eighty years earlier.

The Mormon leaders were particularly enraged by
"exemplary housewife" Sonia Johnson, whom they excommunicated on a variety of questionable charges having to do

with "insubordination"—if not openly stated as such—to the Church patriarchy and undermining its position on the proposed amendment. Particularly galling was Johnson's 1978 tangle with Utah's Senator Orrin Hatch in a Senate committee hearing regarding her avowals of the Church's meddling in the politics of the ERA amendment process. Hatch, himself, was a member of the Church patriarchy and didn't take kindly to Johnson's allegations.[17] Other excommunications followed in the next two decades as the Church began to lose control over the thoughts and writings of its members, particularly the thoughts and writings of a group of intellectuals, the so-called September Six. The Six were excommunicated in the mid-1990s, some for feminist challenges to Church orthodoxy and some for exposing embarrassing incongruities in Church history. These were only some of several excommunications for like reasons that followed soon after.[18]

What exactly were the Church leaders' fears of the ERA in the 1970s? They were already governed under a state constitution that guaranteed the same rights for women with much the same wording. But the leaders immediately turned the intent of the ERA from a legal issue to a *moral* issue. They saw a threat to the family life that the Church had carefully nourished since its repudiation of polygamy at the beginning of the twentieth century. The woman must live out the Church-prescribed domestic ideal, the husband-father to act as the moral authority of the family. The leadership feared that women's liberation—which in their minds espoused homosexuality and abortion, as well as birth control, sexual promiscuity, and intellectual challenges to the Church orthodoxy—would somehow come to be tolerated under the ERA and destroy the domestic bulwark of the Church. It was essential that women guard the home to ensure that Satan could not put such ideas into the heads of their offspring.

Another fear may well have been the thought that women might want to enter the traditionally and exclusively male priesthood, and use their rights under the ERA as their entry. Women were accosting the patriarchy of other Christian churches on this issue, and their initial successes undoubtedly had the Mormon patriarchy worried.

The feminists of the Church were—and no doubt still are—a minority; their push for legal equality for women could not overcome the authority of the Church leaders. The leadership galvanized a far greater number of Mormon women—including members of a Relief Society that once had worked hard for women's rights a century before—to uphold the position of the patriarchy, literally at full shout.[19] Ezra Taft Benson, Quorum president in 1981, gave a perfervid address to the General Conference that year, warning that

> *contrary to conventional wisdom, a mother's place is in the home! I recognize there are voices in our midst that would attempt to convince you that these truths are not applicable to our present-day conditions. If you listen and heed, you will be lured away from your principal obligation.... Some even have been bold enough to suggest that the Church move away from the "Mormon woman stereotype" of homemaking and rearing children. They also say it is wise to limit your family so you can have more time for personal goals and self-fulfillment.*[20]

Such a statement could not be more contrary in essence to the one that Mattie made to the reporter from San Francisco in 1896 when she said that women who can think of something besides cookstoves, washtubs, and baby flannels make the best mothers. And Mattie hoped women would be able to control the number of their children so they could have time for "personal goals and self-fulfillment." Benson's remarks were even contrary to those of President Joseph F. Smith and of the beloved leader, President Brigham Young. Nevertheless Benson's points were effective in Utah and beyond, as the Mormons pushed their position throughout the states that were still in doubt. The ERA amendment died in 1982, failing by three to gain the requisite three-fourths of the states for passage.

In 1987 Benson, who since had become president of the Church, gave almost the same speech as the earlier one, telling women not to curtail the number of their children or postpone having children for "personal or selfish" reasons. Again, mothers belong in the home, not in the workplace. Reporter Peggy Fletcher Stack notes in a *Salt Lake Tribune* article, "Where Have All the Mormon Feminists Gone?" that after this speech "[d]ozens if not hundreds of Mormon women quit their jobs, believing that was what their prophet wanted, while others felt guilty for ignoring that mandate."

An answer to Reporter Stack's question may lie in the response to a 1993 address to top Church staffers by Apostle Boyd Packer, the cerberean guard dog at the temple gates of LDS orthodoxy. Apostle Packer warned of the dangers of "major invasions" by the gay/lesbians, the feminists, and the "so-called scholars or intellectuals."[21]

The late President Hinckley dismissed the feminine dissidents: "I think you'll find our women are very happy now," he said to authors Richard and Joan Ostling, who were working on their book, *Mormon America*, in the late 1990s. "We have a few dissidents. . . . Statistically it's such a very small item that you'd hardly reckon with it."[22]

In the midst of this heated controversy pro and con on feminist issues, the spirit of Martha Hughes Cannon was resurrected from the obscurity of her grave in the Salt Lake City Cemetery. Drawn into the kind of public acclaim that she had experienced in life and then lost almost a century before, Mattie became the subject of a flurry of celebrations honoring her for her accomplishments as a woman doctor, a suffragist, a champion of women's rights, a leader in public health, and for her legacy to the men and women of Utah as a senator of the state.

The first notice was a rather quiet gesture in 1970 by a group of Salt Lake medical organizations, who got together to put a plaque on a stone monument on the corner of South Temple and Second West, near where her little home and office once stood. This was followed in 1984 with the groundbreaking on the $15.8 million Martha Hughes Cannon Public Health Building in Salt Lake City. Also in the 1980s, Mattie was honored with an Endowed Chair in Radiology named after her at the University of Utah School of Medicine.

The 103rd U.S. Congress, in May 1993, introduced Joint House Resolution 207 to issue a commemorative stamp in honor of Dr. Martha Hughes Cannon as the first woman state senator, but the Post Office did not act on the request. And in the historic Salt Lake City-County Building, a portrait of Mattie was hung in Room 335, a conference room that bears her name. The Division of Community and Family Health Services of the Utah Department of Health created the "Martha Hughes Cannon Award" to recognize individuals who have made significant contributions to the health of Utah mothers and children. There is even a musical, *Mattie,* by Nonie Sorenson, that has been produced several times in Saint George, Utah, by players from Utah's Dixie State College. The play celebrates Angus as well as Mattie in that Angus was one of the founders and the first mayor of Saint George.

On July 24, 1996, Governor Mike Leavitt led the crowds of Utah's traditional Pioneer Day celebration into the Utah State Capitol, where an eight-foot statue of Martha Hughes Cannon, created by Utah sculptor Laura Lee Stay, was unveiled in a niche in the rotunda. Mattie's grandson Robert, the last living grandchild to have known her, came from Los Angeles to give the dedication address.[23]

The story of Mattie's life follows many aspects of the story of the Mormon Church itself in the nineteenth and early twentieth centuries; the changes in her expectations of life reflect the changes the Church experienced over the same years. She was a child in the pioneer days of Brigham Young's isolated theocracy—days of ox carts and mud houses, sickness and early death. As President Young began to realize changes would inevitably come to his desert redoubt, he recognized that the role of women would change as well, and he "set them apart" to study and become skilled workers and professionals. This allowed Mattie to receive the education that would sustain her through her entire life and that would in many ways open the world to her. Mormon beliefs about medicine and doctors, about women's work, about marriage, about the society's relationship with the outer world and ultimately with the spiritual world were all in transition, and Mattie's life reflected those changes.[24] Unlike polygamous wives of the past, Mattie had romantic expectations of marriage, but a polygamous marriage could never satisfy her desire for intimacy. She chose for love, but she chose too late. Plural marriage could no longer be sustained in Mormon society. And indeed, given her discredited polygamous marriage, she could never progress as a politician, just as the Church could not integrate into American society until it renounced the "principle." But if she was not to be a politician, then certainly she could pursue her calling as a physician. She maintained her belief in her religion as she challenged and helped to change its attitudes toward women.

Mattie's struggle for women's rights in the late nineteenth century is a struggle that continues today both in this country and abroad. Joelle Kuntz, a reporter for the Paris paper, *Le*

Statue of Dr. Martha Hughes Cannon by sculptor Laura Lee Stay,
installed 1996 in the rotunda of the State Capitol

Temps, wrote in a 2008 article entitled, "L'enjeu" ("The Stake," as in gambling):

> *If the principle of human equality between the genders is virtu-ally a given* [Kuntz is obviously writing about the West], *that of equality of roles and functions is not. There remain great currents of thought in defense of the woman at home, mother exclusively, armed with as many statistical and socio-logical studies as they need to establish their viewpoint.*[25]

Kuntz's remarks acknowledge the progress toward gender equality but suggest changes need to be made in attitudes of equality in women's roles. "Mother exclusively" is precisely what Mattie was arguing against in her many public statements over a hundred years ago.

It is fitting that Martha Hughes Cannon was rediscovered in the late twentieth century, to be revered today in the twenty-first, as a model of achievement both by women of the Church and by women in the greater society who are facing many of the same challenges that she faced, and which she and her sisters did so much to try to overcome a century ago. Yet the direc-tion toward greater rights for women—in which Mattie and her colleagues were moving—was soon countermanded by the Mormon Church, even as changes in laws as well as attitudes toward women's roles outside the Church were progressing. It is to be hoped that Mattie's accomplishments and the hom-age paid to her now will become an inspiration to Mormon and non-Mormon women alike who are seeking to find a balance between belonging to a community of faith, duty to one's fam-ily, and—as President Bensen phrased it so disparagingly—"personal goals and self-fulfillment."

Chronology of Events

Below is the chronology of events in the Mormon Church with special relevance to Martha Hughes Cannon.

1830 – Joseph Smith Jr. establishes Mormon Church (LDS).

1833 – Illinois outlaws polygamy.

1834 – Angus Munn Cannon born in Liverpool, England.

1842 – Angus migrates to America with his siblings and father.

1844 – Joseph Smith Jr. and his brother Hiram murdered in Illinois jail.

1846 – Brigham Young leaves Illinois with first settlers to Utah.

1848 – U.S. acquires Utah from Mexico after Mexican-American War.

1850 – Utah becomes a territory of U.S. Brigham Young appointed territorial governor.

1854 – Angus arrives in Utah.

1857 – Martha Maria Hughes (Mattie) born in Llandudno, Wales. Mountain Meadows massacre takes place in Utah.

1858 – Angus marries Amanda and Sarah Mousley—his first two wives.

1860 – Hughes family migrates to America.

1861 – Abraham Lincoln becomes president; Civil War breaks out; Hughes family arrives in Utah; Peter Hughes (Mattie's father) dies.

1862 – Congress passes Morrill Act outlawing polygamy—not enforced. Mattie's mother marries James Paul.

1870 – Utah women acquire the right to vote.

1875 – Angus marries Clara Mason—his third wife.

1877 – Brigham Young dies.

1880 – John Taylor becomes Church president.

1880 – Mattie receives MD degree from University of Michigan.

1882 – Congress passes the antipolygamy Edmunds Act, enforcing Morrill Act. Mattie receives BS degree from University of Pennsylvania; establishes her medical practice in Salt Lake City.

1884 – Mattie marries Angus Cannon—becoming his fourth wife.

1885 – Elizabeth Rachel Cannon (daughter) born. Angus arrested and jailed for "unlawful cohabitation" under Edmunds Act; released shortly thereafter.

1886 – Mattie and baby Elizabeth leave for exile in England; Angus marries Maria Bennion—his fifth wife.

1887 – Congress passes Edmunds-Tucker Act; Utah women lose the right to vote. U.S. escheats Church properties. Angus marries Johanna Danielson—his sixth wife.

1888 – Mattie and Elizabeth Cannon return to United States.

1890 – Church president Wilford Woodruff issues "Manifesto" outlawing further polygamous marriages by the Church. James Hughes Cannon (son) born.

1893 – Mattie speaks for women's suffrage in Chicago, then to a congressional committee in Washington. Salt Lake Temple completed.

1896 – Utah becomes 45th state. Women's vote restored. Martha Cannon elected first woman state senator in the United States and serves two terms.

1898 – Mattie goes to Washington, D.C., to address Congress about women's suffrage.

1899 – Glendolyn Hughes Cannon (daughter) born. Creates scandal because of Mattie and Angus's polygamous marriage.

1904 – Mormon Church president Joseph Fielding Smith pronounces second manifesto.

1915 – Angus dies. Mattie moves to Los Angeles to work for University of California.

1920 – National women's suffrage Constitutional Amendment.

1923 – Alice Paul introduces Equal Rights Amendment (ERA) to Congress.

1928 – Mattie's daughter Gwendolyn dies at age 29.

1932 – Mattie dies in Los Angeles.

1972 – Congress passes Equal Rights Amendment.

1982 – ERA fails in state legislatures by three states.

1984 – Utah State Public Health Building named in honor of Mattie.

1996 – Statue of Mattie placed in state capitol rotunda.

2008 – Thomas S. Monson becomes current president of the LDS Church.

Notes

Chapter 1

1. *Salt Lake Tribune,* November 1, 1896.

2. *New York Times,* November 1, 1896.

3. Elizabeth McCrimmon, "Dr. Martha Hughes Cannon: First Woman State Senator in America." Unpublished manuscript, no date. Utah State Historical Society.

4. Mormons consider previous baptisms in other branches of Christianity to be invalid.

5. For a general discussion of the Welsh mission, see Kate Carter, "The Mormons from Scotland and Wales" (Salt Lake City, UT: Daughters of Utah Pioneers, 1970).

6. Quoted in Roland D. Dennis, *The Call to Zion: The Story of the First Welsh Emigration,* Religious Studies Center (Provo, UT: Brigham Young University, 1987, p.20). See also Rebecca Bartholomew, *Audacious Women: Early British Mormon Immigrants* (Salt Lake City, UT: Signature Books, 1995).

7. Trail excerpts from "Journal History of the Latter-day Saints," 1861 (access: www.lds.org/churchhistory/library/pioneercompany search/1,15773,3966-1,00.html).

8. Joseph Horne Co. manifest, July 1861, LDS Archives. The following trail events are from journals of the July 1861 Horne Co. travelers who accompanied the Hughes family.

9. Ralph Richards, *Of Medicine, Hospitals, and Doctors* (Salt Lake City, UT: University of Utah Press, 1953, p. 21).

Chapter 2

1. The account of incidents in Mattie's early life comes from the unpublished manuscript by her daughter, Elizabeth Rachel Cannon McCrimmon (no date, Utah State Historical Society). Unfortunately, we don't have Mattie's own diaries. According to Constance Lieber, who discussed the matter with one of Mattie's grandchildren, the diaries were burned by Mattie's son, James, at Mattie's request.

2. Claire Noall, "Superstitions, Customs, and Prescriptions of Mormon Midwives," *California Folklore Quarterly,* v. 3, no. 2 (April 1944, p. 1).

3. Todd Caldecott, "History of Physiomedicalism," *Western Materia Medica* (Wild Rose College of Natural Healing, 2002, p. 2).

4. Chris Enss, *The Doctor Wore Petticoats: Women Physicians of the Old West* (Helena, MT, and Guilford, CT: Two Dot/Globe Pequot, 2006, pp. 112–13).

5. Kate Carter, "And They Were Healed," *Our Pioneer Heritage* (Salt Lake City, UT: Daughters of Utah Pioneers, 1957, p. 80).

6. Christine C. Waters, "Pioneering Women Physicians"; John Sillito, ed., "From College to Market: The Professionalization of Women's Sphere." Papers presented at the Third Annual Meeting of the Utah Women's Association (Salt Lake City, Utah, 1983, p. 47). Find this in Utah Historical Society, *Journal of Discourses,* XIV:109.

7. Seymour Young was at his uncle's bedside when the president died in 1877, apparently of appendicitis. Robert T. Divett, "Medicine and the Mormons," Library of Medical Sciences, University of New Mexico (Albuquerque, NM: 1963, p. 9).

8. Blanche Rose, "Early Utah Medical Practice," *Utah Historical Quarterly* 10 (1942, p. 20). Hereafter, the *Quarterly* will be abbreviated to *UHQ.*

9. Chris Rigby Arrington, "Pioneer Midwives," in Claudia Bushman, ed., *Mormon Sisters: Women in Early Utah* (Cambridge, MA: Emmeline Press, Ltd., 1976, p. 58).

10. Ibid., p. 55.

11. "Pioneering Women Physicians," p. 48.

12. Utah midwives were not certified until 1893.

Chapter 3

1. An interesting documentation of the change in awareness regarding the need for sanitation in surgery is seen in two paintings by American artist Thomas Eakins. In 1875, Eakins painted *The Gross Clinic,* which shows Dr. Samuel Gross supervising a leg surgery at Jefferson Medical College in Philadelphia. The doctor performing the surgery and his students are wearing their street clothes. Fourteen years later in Eakins's 1889 painting, *The Agnew Clinic,* Dr. David Hayes Agnew is instructing students in the performance of a mastectomy, and both doctor and students are clothed in white "scrubs."

2.   Blanche Rose, "Early Utah Medical Practice." After 1896, Dr. Ferguson joined the Theosophists and was excommunicated from the LDS Church.

3.   Mary Roth Walsh, *Doctors Wanted: No Women Need Apply: Sexual Barriers in the Medical Profession, 1835–1975* (New Haven and London: Yale University Press, 1977, p. 180). The first women's medical school, New England Female Medical College, was established in Boston in 1848.

4.   Wilford B. Shaw, ed., *University of Michigan: An Encyclopedic Survey* (Ann Arbor, MI: University of Michigan Press, 1951, pp. 794–95). Quoted in Shari S. Crall, "Something More: A Biography of Martha Hughes Cannon." Unpublished thesis, Brigham Young University, 1985.

5.   *Doctors Wanted: No Women Need Apply,* p. 125, and Mari Graña, *Pioneer Doctor: The Story of a Women's Work* (Guilford, CT: Two Dot/ Globe Pequot, 2006, p. 3).

6.   *Doctors Wanted: No Women Need Apply,* p. 123.

7.   *Marine City Reporter,* reprinted in *Women's Exponent,* August 1, 1881. Quoted in Crall, "Something More: A Biography of Martha Hughes Cannon," p. 17.

8.   Martha Paul Hughes, "Mountain Fever." Unpublished thesis, University of Pennsylvania, 1882. By examining samples of snow from the Rocky Mountains, Mattie determined that the snow contained organic matter blown into the atmosphere during the summer months from malarial swamplands. The organic matter then entered the soil and waterways during winter precipitation. The number of cases of mountain fever declined considerably when people started using water from wells rather than from surface drainages. Mattie's assumption that malaria entered the body through drinking water was ahead of her time. It wasn't until 1889 that the parasite causing malaria was discovered, and not until 1897 that the female anopheles mosquito was identified as the vector. Cf. history of the disease in Robert S. Desowitz, *The Malaria Caper* (New York, W. W. Norton, 1991). A copy of Mattie's handwritten thesis is in this author's possession.

9.   "Dr. Martha Hughes Cannon: First Woman State Senator in America," p. 8.

10.   Martha Hughes Cannon (hereafter MHC) to Barbara Replogle, December 14, 1883, MHC Collection, LDS Archives.

11. Claire Noall, *Guardians of the Hearth* (Bountiful, UT: Horizon Publishers, 1974, p. 155). A discussion of the early Utah hospitals is found in Ralph Richards, MD, *Of Medicine, Hospitals, and Doctors* (Salt Lake City: University of Utah Press, 1953). The Deseret Hospital had no endowment and finally succumbed to lack of funds in the early 1890s. It wasn't until 1905 that another LDS hospital, based on "Mormon regulations," could be established.

12. The First Presidency consists of the Church president, who serves for life, and his two counselors. At the death of the Church president, the president of the Quorum of the Twelve is next in line for the presidency.

13. *Guardians of the Hearth,* p. 146.

Chapter 4

1. William W. Slaughter, *Life in Zion: An Intimate Look at the Latter-day Saints, 1820–1995* (Salt Lake City, UT: Deseret Book Co., 1995, p. 12). Governor Lilburn A. Boggs's Order stated: "The Mormons must be treated as enemies, and must be exterminated or driven from the state for the public good." In an ironic twist of history, the governor's great-grandson, Alvah Boggs, joined the LDS Church in 1956 and publicly repudiated his great-grandfather. Missouri governor Christopher S. Bond, in a statement to celebrate freedom of religion in the bicentennial year, finally rescinded the Order on June 25, 1976.

2. D. Michael Quinn, *The Mormon Hierarchy: Origins of Power* (Salt Lake City, UT: Signature Books, 1994, p. 181).

3. Carrel Hilton Sheldon, "Mormon Haters," in Claudia Bushman, ed., *Mormon Sisters: Women in Early Utah* (Logan, UT: Utah State University Press, 1997, p. 113).

4. Quoted in Julie Roy Jeffrey, *Frontier Women* (New York: Hill and Wang, 1979, p. 181).

5. Gustav O. Larson, "Utah and the Civil War," *UHQ*, Winter 1965, p. 181.

6. Todd Compton, *In Sacred Loneliness: The Plural Wives of Joseph Smith* (Salt Lake City, UT: Deseret Book Co., 2008). Quinn estimates that Young had closer to fifty-two wives (cf. *The Mormon Hierarchy,* pp. 607–8).

7. Robert Wright, *The Moral Animal* (New York: Vintage, 1994, pp. 90–94).

8. Governor S. S. Harding to William Seward, September 3, 1862. Quoted in "Utah and the Civil War," p. 68.

9. Stephen Cresswell, "The U.S. Department of Justice in Utah Territory, 1870–1890," *UHQ* 53:3, Summer 1985, p. 211.

10. D. Michael Quinn, *The Mormon Hierarchy: Extensions of Power.* Chronological list of events in Mormon history (access: www.i4m .com/think/history/mormon_history.htm). Ten dollars would be worth about $220 in today's currency.

11. Patricia L. Scott and Linda Thatcher, eds., *Women in Utah History: Paradigm or Paradox?* (Logan, UT: Utah State University Press, 2005, p. 44).

12. *98 US 145 (1878).*

13. Ibid.

14. Mark Twain, *Roughing It* (Hartford, CT: American Publishing Co., 1872, p. I:101, 117).

15. Iving Wallace. *The Twenty-seventh Wife.* Quoted in Jessica Longaker "The Role of Women in Mormonism," March 27, 1995 (access: www.exmormon.org/mormwomn.html).

16. Irving Wallace, *The Twenty-seventh Wife* (New York: Simon & Schuster, 1961, p. 101).

17. In current dollars, $10,333 and $6,200 respectively.

18. D. Michael Quinn, "LDS Church Authority and New Plural Marriages, 1890–1904," *Dialogue: A Journal of Mormon Thought, Part 3* (Spring, 1985), hereafter shortened to *Dialogue.*

19. The Endowment House was a venue used for weddings and other rituals before the Salt Lake Temple was completed.

Chapter 5

1. MHC to Barbara Replogle, November 2, 1884. All letters to Replogle quoted here are part of the MHC Collection, LDS Archives.

2. MHC to Barbara Replogle, May 1, 1885.

3. *115 U.S. 55, 6 S Ct. 278*

4. *Deseret News,* January 28, 1885.

5. Quoted in Nancy Driggs, "Victims of the Conflict," in *Mormon Sisters: Women in Early Utah,* p. 117.

6. Angus Munn Cannon, "Journal" (hereafter AMC Journal), May 9, 1885. Special Collections, Brigham Young University (hereafter BYU).

7. AMC Journal, June 9, 1885.

8. MHC to Barbara Replogle, May 1, 1894.

9. AMC Journal, August 26, 1885.

10. Ken Driggs, "The Prosecutions Begin: Defining Cohabitation in 1885," *Dialogue* v. 21, no.1, 1988, pp. 109–24.

11. James B. Allen and Glen M. Leonard, *The Story of the Latter-day Saints* (Salt Lake City, UT: Deseret Book Co., 1976, p. 409).

12. Jeffrey Nichols, *Prostitution, Politics, and Power: Salt Lake City, 1847–1918* (Urbana and Chicago: University of Illinois Press, 2002, p. 1).

13. "The U.S. Department of Justice in Utah Territory, 1870–1890," p. 216.

14. Ibid.

15. Melinda Evans, "Belva Lockwood and the Mormon Question." Unpublished manuscript, BYU, 1999.

16. Quoted in Donald Q. Cannon, "Angus M. Cannon: Pioneer, President, Patriarch," in Donald Q. Cannon and David J. Whittaker, eds., *Supporting Saints: Life Stories of Nineteenth-Century Mormons,* Religious Studies Center (Provo, UT: BYU, 1985, p. 389).

17. MHC to AMC, March 1886. All letters between MHC and AMC quoted here are from the AMC Collection in the LDS Archives, and published in Constance Lieber and John Sillito, *Letters from Exile* (Salt Lake City, UT: Signature Books, 1899), unless otherwise noted.

Chapter 6

1. Beatrice Evans and Janath R. Cannon, *Cannon Family Historical Treasury,* 2nd Ed., George Cannon Family Association (Salt Lake City, UT: Publishers Press, 1995, p. 215).

2. "Angus M. Cannon: Pioneer, President, Patriarch," p. 369.

3. "Dr. Martha Hughes Cannon: First Woman State Senator in America," p. 8.

4. AMC Journal, April 16, 1906. Quoted in "Angus M. Cannon: Pioneer, President, Patriarch," p. 395.

5. AMC Journal, March 23, 1886, Special Collections, BYU.

6.   AMC Journal, July 5, 1886.

7.   AMC to MHC, November 16, 1887.

8.   MHC to AMC, March 25, 1886.

9.   MHC to AMC, April 29, 1886.

10. MHC to AMC, February 5, 1888.

11. MHC to AMC, June 6, 1886.

12. MHC to AMC, June 6, 1886.

13. MHC to AMC, January 28, 1887.

14. MHC to AMC, August 29, 1886.

15. "Mrs. Hull" was Anna Balmer Meyer.

16. MHC to AMC, April 5, 1887.

17. MHC to AMC, September 16, 1887.

18. MHC to AMC, November 3, 1887.

19. AMC to MHC, November 16, 1887.

20. MHC to AMC, December 11, 1887.

Chapter 7

1.   "The U.S. Department of Justice in Utah Territory, 1870–1890,"
     p. 215.

2.   *The Story of the Latter-day Saints,* chapter 13. See also Rollin Lynde
     Hartt, "The Mormons," *Atlantic Monthly,* February 1900.

3.   "Angus M. Cannon: Pioneer, President, Patriarch," p. 393.

4.   MHC to AMC, January 15, 1888.

5.   MHC to AMC, February 3, 1888.

6.   MHC to AMC, February 5, 1888. Liolin was a suitor of Mattie's,
     who left school in despair because she wouldn't marry him.

7.   MHC to AMC, March 19, 1988.

8.   MHC to AMC, April 8, 1988.

9.   MHC to Replogle, September 18, 1884, MHC Collection,
     LDS Archives.

10. MHC to Replogle, November 2, 1884, MHC Collection.

11. MHC to Replogle, August 6, 1887, MHC Collection.

12. MHC to Replogle, August 10, 1888, MHC Collection.

13. MHC to AMC, June 8, 1888, in *Letters from Exile.*

14. MHC to AMC, no date (late 1888).

15. "Dr. Martha Hughes Cannon: First Woman State Senator in America," p. 12.

16. MHC to AMC, December 30, 1891, MHC Collection.

17. MHC to Replogle, June 6, 1891, MHC Collection.

Chapter 8

1. "LDS Church Authority and New Plural Marriages, 1890–1904," Part 4.

2. Stanley Ivins, "Notes on Mormon Polygamy," in D. Michael Quinn, ed., *The New Mormon History: Revisionist Essays on the Past* (Salt Lake City, UT: Signature, 1994, pp. 170, 179). Ivins notes, "The Saints accepted plurality in theory, but most of them were loath to put it into practice, despite continual urging of leaders in whose divine authority they had the utmost faith. . . . Left to itself undisturbed by pressure from without, the Church would inevitably have given up the practice of polygamy, perhaps even sooner than it did under pressure."

3. Richard S. Van Wagoner, *Mormon Polygamy: A History* (Salt Lake City, UT: Signature, 1989, p. 143).

4. D. Michael Quinn comments in his article, "LDS Church Authority and New Plural Marriages, 1890–1904," that while the leaders claimed a unanimous vote, the majority of the people were too shocked to vote.

5. Davis Bitton, *The Ritualization of Mormon History and Other Essays* (Urbana and Chicago: University of Illinois Press, 1994, p. 137).

6. *Mormon Polygamy: A History,* p. 150.

7. Driggs, Nancy, "Victims of the Conflict," in C. Bushman, ed., *Mormon Sisters: Women in Early Utah* (Logan, UT: Utah State University Press, 1997, p. 147).

8. *The Story of the Latter-day Saints,* p. 416.

9. *Mormon Polygamy: A History,* pp. 160–62.

10. Kate Carter, ed., "Pioneer Women Doctors," *Our Pioneer Heritage* (Salt Lake City, UT: Daughters of Utah Pioneers, v. I, p. 383).

Chapter 9

1. Katherine L. MacKay, "Chronology of Woman's Suffrage in Utah," in Carol C. Madsen, ed., *Battle for the Ballot* (Logan, UT: Utah State University Press, 1997, p. 311).

2. *Mormon Polygamy: A History*, p. 96. Emmeline Wells was the seventh plural wife of Elder Daniel Wells of the First Presidency. She was disliked by his other wives and lived separately from them. She wrote in her diary: "O, if only my husband could love me even a little and not seem to be perfectly indifferent to any sensation of that kind."

3. Letter from S. B. Anthony to Susa Young Gates, quoted in Joan Iverson, "The Mormon Suffrage Relationship," in *Battle for the Ballot*, p. 166.

4. *Chicago Daily Tribune*, May 26, 1893.

5. "Pioneering Women Physicians," p. 51.

6. *Chicago Record*, May 15, 1893.

7. "A Woman's Assembly Address," *Woman's Exponent*, April 1, 1894, p. 114. Cited in "Something More: A Biography of Martha Hughes Cannon," p. 66.

8. Jean Bickmore White, "Woman's Place is in the Constitution," in *Battle for the Ballot*, p. 223.

9. Maureen Ursenbach Beecher, Carol C. Madsen, Jill Mulvay Derr, "The Latter-day Saints and Women's Rights, 1870–1920," *Battle for the Ballot*, p. 99.

Chapter 10

1. *The Story of the Latter-day Saints*, p. 418.

2. Allen Kent Powell, *Utah History Encyclopedia* (Salt Lake City: University of Utah Press, 1994). Heber Grant would later become president of the Church in 1918.

3. Carol C. Madsen, "Schism in the Sisterhood," *Battle for the Ballot*, p. 257.

4. Diary of Abraham Cannon, June 18, 1894, LDS Archives.

5. *Salt Lake Tribune*, October 12, 1896.

6. *Battle for the Ballot*, p. 265.

Chapter 11

1. *Deseret News,* July 26, 1871. Quoted in Maureen U. Beecher, "Eliza R. Snow," in V. Burgess-Olson, ed., *Sister Saints* (Provo, UT: Brigham Young University Press, 1978, p. 15).

2. Harriet H. Arrington, "Alice Merrill Horne: Art Pioneer and Early Utah Legislator," *UHQ* 58:3, p. 268.

3. Ibid.

4. Diary of Priddy Meeks, quoted in *Guardians of the Hearth,* p. 18.

5. *Utah Public Documents: 1897–98 and 1899–1900,* Section 22, Report of the Board of Health. Perhaps one example of this resistance to forming local boards of health is Toole County, whose board was established under Mattie's 1896 enabling legislation, but not until 1982.

6. *Of Medicine, Hospitals, and Doctors,* p. 45.

7. *Deseret News,* February 7, 1901.

8. Claire Noall, "Medicine among the Early Mormons," *Western Folklore* v. 18 (April 1953, p. 162).

9. A famous carrier of the disease was the Irish immigrant, Mary Mallon. Although seemingly healthy herself, as a cook she unwittingly spread typhoid in several New York households and businesses in the early twentieth century. A similar situation occurred in Salt Lake City in 1923, when an infected woman worked in a popular delicatessen. Unlike Mallon, this woman was sick, but kept on working. At least 188 cases—and 13 deaths—were traced to the delicatessen, but there may have been many more among tourists who became ill after they left the state.

10. The following letters are from the Angus M. Cannon Collection in the LDS Archives.

11. MHC to AMC, March 1885, LDS Archives.

12. David Shannon, ed., *Beatrice Webb's American Diary, 1898* (Madison: University of Wisconsin Press, 1963, pp. 130–35).

13. *Utah History Encyclopedia.* See Thatcher, Moses.

14. *Salt Lake Tribune,* February 2, 1897.

15. *Utah History Encyclopedia.* See Thatcher, Moses.

Chapter 12

1. "Dr. Martha Hughes Cannon: First Woman State Senator in America," p. 16.

2. Hearing on House Joint Resolution 68, February 15, 1898.

3. MHC to Emmeline Wells, February 27, 1898, cited in "Dr. Martha Hughes Cannon: First Woman State Senator in America," p. 17.

4. *San Francisco Examiner*, November 8, 1896. Although the Church has maintained a stand against birth control until the present day, later acknowledging its use for health reasons only, it's clear that modern Mormons do use methods of birth control. In his 1976 article on the subject, Lester E. Bush Jr. cites a 1972 survey of 132 Salt Lake City LDS families that shows 83 percent used birth control methods as opposed to 17 percent that did not. Of 543 single BYU students surveyed in 1971, 84 percent said they would use it for the wife's health, but only 21 percent to avoid additional children. Lester E. Bush Jr., "Birth Control among the Mormons: Introduction to an Insistent Question," *Dialogue* v. 10, no. 2 (Autumn 1976, pp. 12–44).

5. AMC Collection, LDS Archives.

6. *Salt Lake Tribune*, July 27, 1899.

7. Ibid., July 9, 1899. The scandal was bruited about far and wide. The July 8, 1899, issue of the *New York Evening Journal* carried the headline BABY CAUSES A SUIT FOR POLYGAMY AGAINST CHIEF MORMON. Some reporters anticipated a "raid" like those that took place during the prosecutions under the Edmunds-Tucker Act. For example, the Jamestown, WI, *Daily Gazette* of July 10, 1899, reported: "The arrest of President Cannon is the first step in a raid that is to be instituted against polygamists, and some stirring times are expected." The *Gazette* also noted that B. H. Roberts "will not be arrested until just before Congress meets in December next, in order that it may be pending when the question of expelling him comes up."

8. Ibid.

9. Ibid., July 19, 1899.

10. *New York Times*, December 21, 1898. Fanny Stenhouse was the author of *Tell It All*. See also *New York Times*, November 10, 1899, which reports the resolution favoring an amendment to the Constitution to outlaw polygamy.

11. *Deseret Evening News*, February 10, 1900. In today's currency, $100 would be worth approximately $2,500.

12. *Journal of Discourses,* v. 13, p. 102. Edward Gibbon, in his many-tomed analysis of the decline of Rome, apparently missed this point.

13. *Mormon Hierarchy: Extensions of Power* (access: www.lds-mormon .com/post_manifesto_polygamy.shtml). Quinn quotes historian Ken Cannon as estimating 250 post-Manifesto marriages, including ten plural marriages among the General Authorities. The first was Apostle John W. Taylor, son of the late president, who married on October 10, 1890, four days after the Manifesto was ratified in the General Conference. Later, Taylor and Apostle Matthias Cowley, both of whom officiated at several polygamous marriages, resigned from the Twelve because they were "out of harmony" with the Church. Their resignations were intended to lift pressure from the Smoot investigation. Subsequently, Cowley was disfellowshipped and Taylor excommunicated. Many felt the two were scapegoats. See *Mormon Polygamy: A History,* p. 180.

14. *Mormon Hierarchy: Extensions of Power* (access: www.lds-mormon .com/post_manifesto_polygamy.shtml). See also Chronology of Mormon History (access: www.i4m.com/think/history/mormon _history.htm).

15. Ibid. In April 1919 a stake president wrote that the Church members were complaining "on account of so many Smiths being chosen," although by this time Joseph F. Smith had died.

16. Ibid.

17. Ibid.

18. Donald Q. Cannon, "Angus M. Cannon: Pioneer, President, Patriarch," in *Supporting Saints: Life Stories of Nineteenth-Century Mormons,* pp. 304–6.

19. MHC to AMC, September 11, 1904, AMC Collection, LDS Archives.

20. MHC to AMC, December 2, 1904.

21. MHC to AMC, October 2, 1906.

22. Elizabeth Rachel Cannon to AMC, December 28, 1906.

23. *Mormon Polygamy: A History,* p. 173. B. Carmon Hardy has pointed out in his book, *Solemn Covenant: The Mormon Polygamous Passage* (Urbana, IL: University of Illinois Press, 1992, pp. 365–78) that the Saints interpreted anti-Mormon laws as satanic artifice in which they had become involuntarily ensnared. They were forced to make promises to the government; therefore, they did not consider the words binding.

24. Proceedings Before the Committee on Privileges and Elections of the United States, April 21, 1904.

25. Frank J. Cannon and Harvey J. Higgins, *Under the Prophet in Utah* (Boston: C. M. Clark, 1911, chapter 13).

26. See "LDS Church Authority in New Plural Marriages, 1890–1904," p. 1 of Part 1.

27. Ibid., and also *Under the Prophet in Utah*, chapter 13.

28. In today's currency, $300 would be worth approximately $7,154.

Chapter 13

1. Kenneth Cannon II, "After the Manifesto: Mormon Polygamy 1890–1906," in Quinn, ed., *The New Mormon History*.

2. *Under the Prophet in Utah*, chapter 17.

3. *Of Medicine, Hospitals, and Doctors*, p. 80.

4. Diaries of Emmeline Wells (1905), LDS Archives. I am indebted to Constance Lieber for pointing out this diary entry.

5. *Salt Lake Herald*, April 14, 1906.

6. *Salt Lake Herald*, June 29, 1904.

7. *The Sanitarian*, v. 48, p. 358.

8. Elizabeth Rachel to AMC, March 4, 1912, LDS Archives. Clark Bell, A. W. Herzog, *Medico-Legal Journal*, v. 28, no. 4 (1911). The U.S. tuberculosis mortality rate in 1901 was 200/100,000. By 1950 the rate had been reduced to 26/100,000. Although the U.S. rate had been reduced to 4.6/100,000 by 2006, the worldwide rate has actually increased greatly today, particularly in Africa, where drug-resistant strains combine with the HIV-positive condition.

9. *Deseret News*, June 7, 1915, obituary of Angus Munn Cannon.

10. Robert F. Daniel, *American Philanthropy in the Near East, 1820–1960* (Athens, OH: Ohio University Press, 1971, pp. 166–70).

11. The 1920 U.S. Census lists Mattie, Gwendolyn, and Elizabeth Rachel and her children living at the ranch. However, Mattie had already started working for the University of California. Her name is listed in the 1918 medical personnel directory for the university at James's address, 4034 Homer Street in Los Angeles (*Los Angeles Medical Department Register*, University of California, Berkeley, 1918, p. 163).

Chapter 14

1. University of California, Los Angeles Medical Department. Report to the President of the University, Dean W. Jarvis Barlow, July 1, 1912. This gives a description of the Selwyn Emmett Graves Memorial Dispensary, where Mattie later worked. The National Library of Medicine in Bethesda, Maryland, has no record of any publications by Mattie.

2. *Salt Lake Tribune,* February 6, 1927.

3. Elizabeth McCrimmon, "James Hughes Cannon." Unpublished manuscript, LDS Archives.

4. *Salt Lake Tribune,* July 10, 1932, obituary of Martha Hughes Cannon.

5. *Journal of Discourses,* 18:37.

6. Annie Laurie Black, "Our Woman Senator," *San Francisco Examiner,* November 8, 1896. Reprinted in the *Salt Lake Herald,* November 11, 1896.

7. Quoted in Vee Carlisle, "Women in Utah History." An address for National Women's History Month (1994, Utah Historical Society, p. 3). Carlisle also notes that Quentin Cannon, Mattie's grandson in the House of Representatives, voted against the ERA. She asks: "What would Mattie be thinking . . . ?"

8. Muriel Ursenbach Beecher, "Eliza R. Snow," in *Sister Saints,* p. 11.

9. "Our Woman Senator."

10. Quoted in Leonard J. Arrington and Davis Bitton, *The Mormon Experience: History of the Latter-day Saints* (New York: Alfred Knopf, 1979, p. 222). From "Relief Society Minute Book," April 28, 1842, LDS Archives.

11. Brigham Young, *Discourses.* Quoted in "Medicine among the Early Mormons," p. 160.

12. Linda King Newell, "A Gift Given, A Gift Taken: Anointing and Blessing the Sick among Mormon Women," in *The New Mormon History,* pp. 114–16.

13. Church of Jesus Christ of Latter-day Saints, "A Brief Statement of Principles of the Gospel" (Salt Lake City, 1943). Quoted in "Medicine and the Mormons," p. 2.

14. "A Gift Given, A Gift Taken," p. 116.

15. *The Mormon Experience: History of the Latter-day Saints*, p. 233. See also Jesse L. Embry, "Grain Storage: The Balance of Power between Priesthood Authority and Relief Society Autonomy," *Dialogue* 15 (Winter 1982, pp. 59–66). Embry discusses the gradual takeover of the women's grain storage program.

16. Martha Sonntag Bradley, *Pedestals and Podiums: Utah Women, Religious Authority, and Equal Rights* (Salt Lake City, UT: Signature Books, 2007, p. 69 et seq.). The following discussion of the effects of the Women's Movement and the ERA on the Mormon patrimony is largely taken from Bradley's book.

17. Sonia Johnson, *From Housewife to Heretic* (Garden City, NY: Anchor Books, 1983, pp. 133–36). A memoir of the events leading to her excommunication. Johnson was nominated for president of the United States by the leftist Citizens Party in 1984, the same year that another woman, Geraldine Ferraro, was Walter Mondale's running mate. In 2000 Orrin Hatch tried for the Republican nomination against George W. Bush.

18. "Exiles in Zion," *Salt Lake Tribune*, August 16, 2003. This article provides a ten-year perspective on the "September Six" excommunications. One of the Six has been reinstated, while one is still disfellowshipped rather than excommunicated. One of the Six, Maxine Hanks, was excommunicated for, among other things, advocating that the priesthood be opened to women.

19. *Pedestals and Podiums*, p. vii. Bradley relates her experience at the 1977 International Women's Year meeting in Salt Lake City. Nearly every proposal was shouted down by a mob of anti-ERA Mormon women.

20. Ezra Taft Benson, quoted in *Pedestals and Podiums*, p. 72.

21. Peggy Fletcher Stack, "Where Have All the Mormon Feminists Gone?" *Salt Lake Tribune* (access: www.beliefnet.com/story135 __13568). Apostle Boyd Packer's address noted in Richard N. Ostling and Joan Ostling, *Mormon America: The Power and the Promise* (New York: HarperCollins Publishers, 1999, p. 364).

22. *Mormon America*, p. 364. As to how happy Mormon women are, LDS psychologist Kent Ponder, in a 2003 Internet article entitled "Mormon Women, Prozac, and Therapy" (access: http://packham .n4m.org/prozac.htm), discusses the fact that Utah has the highest percentage of antidepressant drug use (primarily Prozac) of any state, and that women's use is far higher than men's. Dr. Ponder

interviewed 300 Mormon women regarding their purchase of antidepressants. He comments, "It is difficult to be emotionally detached from the horrendous mental anguish experienced by so many entirely innocent Mormon women, as reflected in their rate of purchase of antidepressants. . . . Forceful language may be helpful, even necessary, to jar LDS men's consciousness into a state of greater awareness, hopefully breaking through their/our habitual LDS-cultural view of LDS women."

23. Mattie's statue joined a bust of her old friend Emmeline Wells, along with those of Maurice Warshaw and Governor Simon Bamberger, in the rotunda niches. At this writing, Mattie and her fellow statues are still in storage while the renovation of the capitol building is completed. Bronze characters representing Land and Community, Emigration, Technology, and Arts and Education now occupy the renovated rotunda niches. Mattie will be moved to preside over the entrance to the senate chamber in the East Building.

24. In 1962 a study was made of LDS attitudes toward polygamy. Eighty-two females and seventy-two males were randomly chosen from the married population of a small Mormon town (pop. 1,000). Approximately two-thirds of the interviewees stated that they approved of the polygynous practices of their early forebears. Forty-nine percent stated that now they would not consider polygyny under any circumstances; 40 percent stated they would consider it if God commanded them through their prophets; and 6 percent replied they didn't know. Ninety-two percent responded that they disapproved of polygyny (in 1963), while the remaining 8 percent had no opinion. There were no significant differences in the attitudes of the men and women. John R. Christianson, "Contemporary Mormons' Attitudes toward Polygamist Practices," *Marriage and Family Living*, v. 25 (May 1963).

25. Joelle Kuntz, "L'enjeu," *Le Temps*, January 17, 2008.

Bibliography

Abbott, Delila M. "Women Legislators of Utah, 1896–1976." Unpublished manuscript (Salt Lake City: Utah State Historical Society, no date).

Allen, James B., and Glen M. Leonard. *The Story of the Latter-day Saints* (Salt Lake City, UT: Deseret Book Company, 1976).

Anthony, Susan B., and Ida Husted Harper, eds. *The History of Woman's Suffrage* (Rochester, NY: Susan B. Anthony, 1902).

Arrington, Chris Rigby. "Pioneer Midwives," in Claudia L. Bushman, ed., *Mormon Sisters: Women in Early Utah* (Logan, UT: Utah State University Press, 1997).

Arrington, Harriet H. "Alice Merrill Horne, Art Pioneer and Early Utah Legislator," *Utah Historical Quarterly* 58:3.

Arrington, Leonard J., and Davis Bitton. *The Mormon Experience: History of the Latter-day Saints* (New York: Alfred Knopf, 1979).

Bartholomew, Rebecca. *Audacious Women: Early British Mormon Immigrants* (Salt Lake City, UT: Signature Books, 1995).

Beecher, Muriel Ursenbach. "Eliza R. Snow," in Vicky Burgess-Olson, ed., *Sister Saints* (Provo, UT: Brigham Young University Press, 1978).

Beeton, Beverly. "Women Vote in the West, 1869–1896," in C. Madsen, ed., *Battle for the Ballot* (Logan, UT: Utah State University Press, 1997).

Bell, Clark, and A. W. Herzog, eds. *Medico-Legal Journal*, v. 28, no. 4 (1911).

Bitton, Davis. *The Ritualization of Mormon History and Other Essays* (Urbana and Chicago: University of Illinois Press, 1994).

Black, Annie Laurie. "Our Woman Senator," *San Francisco Examiner,* November 8, 1896.

Book of Abraham Project. Web site containing diaries of Joseph Smith contemporaries, *Doctrine and Covenants, Book of Mormon,* and other scriptures (www.boap.org).

Bradley, Martha Sonntag. *Pedestals and Podiums: Utah Women, Religious Authority, and Equal Rights* (Salt Lake City, UT: Signature Books, 2007).

Burgess-Olson, Vicky, ed. *Sister Saints* (Provo, UT: Brigham Young University Press, 1978).

Bush, Lester E. Jr. "Birth Control among the Mormons: Introduction to an Insistent Question," *Dialogue: A Journal of Mormon Thought,* v. 10, no. 2 (Autumn 1976).

Bushman, Claudia L. "Mystics and Healers," in Claudia Bushman, ed., *Mormon Sisters: Women in Early Utah* (Logan, UT: Utah State University Press, 1997).

Caldecott, Todd. "History of Physiomedicalism," *Western Materia Medica* (Wild Rose College of Natural Healing, 2002).

Cannon vs. United States. 116 U.S. 55, 6 S. Ct. 278.

Cannon, Angus Munn, Collection. LDS Archives.

———. Diary. Special Collections, Brigham Young University, Provo, Utah.

———. "The Edmunds Law: 'Unlawful Cohabitation' as Defined by Chief Justice Charles S. Zane." (Salt Lake City, Trial: April 27–29, 1885).

Cannon, Donald Q. "Angus M. Cannon: Pioneer, President, Patriarch," in Donald Q. Cannon and David Whittaker, eds., *Supporting Saints: Life Stories of Nineteenth-Century Mormons,* Religious Studies Center (Provo, UT: Brigham Young University, 1985).

Cannon, Frank J., and Harvey J. Higgins. *Under the Prophet in Utah* (Boston: C. M. Clark, 1911).

Cannon, Kenneth II. "After the Manifesto: Mormon Polygamy 1890–1906," in D. Michael Quinn, ed., *The New Mormon History: Revisionist Essays on the Past* (Salt Lake City, UT: Signature Books, 1992).

Cannon, Martha Hughes, Collection. LDS Archives.

Carlisle, Vee. "Women in Utah History," an address for National Women's History Month. Unpublished manuscript (Utah Historical Society, 1994).

Carter, Kate B. "And They Were Healed," *Our Pioneer Heritage* (Salt Lake City, UT: Daughters of Utah Pioneers, 1957).

———. "The Mormons from Scotland and Wales," *Our Pioneer Heritage* (Salt Lake City, UT: Daughters of Utah Pioneers, 1970).

———. "Pioneer Woman Doctors," *Our Pioneer Heritage* (Salt Lake City, UT: Daughters of Utah Pioneers, 1958–74).

Chicago Record. Cf. endnotes for specific dates and references.

Christiansen, John R. "Contemporary Mormons' Attitude toward Polygamist Practice," *Marriage and Family Living,* v. 25 (May 1963).

Compton, Todd. *In Sacred Loneliness: The Plural Wives of Joseph Smith* (Salt Lake City, UT: Deseret Book Co., 2008).

Crall, Shari Siebers. "Something More: A Biography of Martha Hughes Cannon." Unpublished BA Thesis (Brigham Young University, 1985).

Cresswell, Stephen. "The U.S. Department of Justice in Utah Territory, 1870–1890," *Utah Historical Quarterly* v. 53:3 (Summer 1985).

Daniel, Robert F. *American Philanthropy in the Near East, 1820–1960* (Athens, OH: Ohio University Press, 1971).

Dennis, Ronald D. *The Call to Zion: The Story of the First Welsh Emigration,* Religious Studies Center (Provo, UT: Brigham Young University, 1987).

Derr, Jill M., Janath R. Cannon, and Maureen U. Beecher. *Women of the Covenant: The Story of the Relief Society* (Salt Lake City, UT: Deseret Book Co., 1992).

Deseret Evening News. Cf. endnotes for specific dates and references.

Desowitz, Robert S. *The Malaria Caper* (New York: W. W. Norton, 1991).

Divett, Robert T. "Medicine and the Mormons," *Bulletin of the Medical Library Association* 51 (January 1963).

Driggs, Ken. "The Prosecutions Begin: Defining Cohabitation in 1885," *Dialogue: A Journal of Mormon Thought,* v. 21, no. 1 (1988).

Driggs, Nancy. "Victims of the Conflict," in Claudia Bushman, ed., *Mormon Sisters: Women in Early Utah* (Logan, UT: Utah State University Press, 1997).

Embry, Jessie L. "Grain Storage: The Balance of Power between Priesthood Authority and Relief Society Autonomy," *Dialogue: A Journal of Mormon Thought,* 15 (Winter 1982).

Enss, Chris. *The Doctor Wore Petticoats: Women Physicians of the Old West* (Helena, MT, and Guilford, CT: Two Dot/Globe Pequot, 2006).

Evans, Beatrice Cannon, and Janath Russell Cannon. *Cannon Family Historical Treasury,* 2nd ed. George Cannon Family Association (Salt Lake City, UT: Publishers Press, 1995).

Evans, Melinda. "Belva Lockwood and the Mormon Question." Unpublished manuscript (Brigham Young University, 1999).

Exiles in Zion," *Salt Lake Tribune,* August 16, 2003.

Flexnor, Eleanor, and Ellen Fitzpatrick. *Century of Struggle: The Woman's Rights Movement in the United States* (Cambridge, MA: Harvard University Press, 1959).

Goldstein, Laurie. *New York Times,* June 11, 2007.

Graña, Mari. *Pioneer Doctor: The Story of a Woman's Work* (Helena, MT, and Guilford, CT: Two Dot/Globe Pequot, 2006).

Hardy, B. Carmon. *Solemn Covenant: The Mormon Polygamy Passage* (Urbana, IL: University of Illinois Press, 1992).

Hartt, Rollin Lynde. "The Mormons," *Atlantic Monthly,* February 1900.

Heinemann, Sue. *Timelines of American Women's History* (New York: Berkeley Publishing Group, 1996).

Hughes, Martha Paul. "Mountain Fever." Unpublished BA Thesis (University of Pennsylvania, 1882).

Iverson, Joan. "Feminist Implications of Mormon Polygamy," *Feminist Studies* v. 10, no. 3 (Fall 1984).

———. "The Mormon Suffrage Relationship," in Carol C. Madsen, ed., *Battle for the Ballot* (Logan, UT: Utah State University, 1997).

Ivins, Stanley. "Notes on Mormon Polygamy," in D. Michael Quinn, ed., *The New Mormon History: Revisionist Essays on the Past* (Salt Lake City, UT: Signature Books, 1994).

Jeffrey, Julie Roy. *Frontier Women* (New York: Hill and Wang, 1979).

Jensen, Andrew. *Latter-day Saints' Biographical Encyclopedia* (Salt Lake City, UT: Andrew Jensen History Co., 1901–1936).

Johnson, Sonia. *From Housewife to Heretic* (Garden City, NY: Anchor Books, 1983).

Kunz, Joelle. "L'enjeu," *Le Temps,* January 17, 2008.

Larson, Gustav O. "The Crusade and the Manifesto," in Richard D. Poll et al., eds., *Utah's History* (Provo, UT: Brigham Young University Press, 1978).

———. "Utah and the Civil War," *Utah Historical Quarterly* (Winter 1965).

A Legacy Remembered: The Relief Society Magazine, 1914–1970 (Salt Lake City, UT: Deseret Books, 1982).

Lieber, Constance L. "The Goose Hangs High," *Utah Historical Quarterly* v. 48, no. 1 (Winter 1980).

Lieber, Constance L., and John Sillito. *Letters from Exile: The Correspondence of Martha Hughes Cannon and Angus M. Cannon, 1886–1888* (Salt Lake City, UT: Signature Books, 1989).

MacKay, Katherine L. "Chronology of Woman's Suffrage in Utah," in Carol C. Madsen, ed., *Battle for the Ballot* (Logan, UT: Utah State University Press, 1997).

Madsen, Carol Cornwall, ed. *Battle for the Ballot: Essays on Woman's Suffrage in Utah, 1870–1896* (Logan, UT: Utah State University Press, 1997).

———. "Schism in the Sisterhood," in Carol Madsen, ed., *Battle for the Ballot* (Logan, UT: Utah State University Press, 1997).

McCrimmon, Elizabeth C. "Dr. Martha Hughes Cannon, First Woman Senator." Unpublished manuscript (Utah State Historical Society, no date).

———. "James Hughes Cannon." Unpublished manuscript (LDS Archives, no date).

Medico-Legal Society of New York. *The Sanitarian,* v. 48 (New York: Barnes & Co., 1902).

Meyer, Sandra L. *Western Women and the Frontier Experience, 1800–1915* (Albuquerque, NM: University of New Mexico Press, 1982).

Mormon Pioneer Overland Travel (www.lds.org/churchhistory/library/pioneercompanysearch/1,15773,3966-1,00.html).

Mormon Women's Protest: An Appeal for Freedom, Justice and Equal Rights, Salt Lake City, Utah, 1886 (www.fairlds.org/Misc/Introduction_to_Mormon_Womens_Protest.html).

Morrell, Joseph R. *Utah's Health and You: A History of Utah's Public Health* (Salt Lake City, UT: Deseret Book Co., 1956).

Mulford, Karen Surina. *Trailblazers: Twenty Amazing Western Women* (Flagstaff, AZ: Northland Publishing Co., 2001).

Newell, Linda King. "A Gift Given, A Gift Taken: Anointing and Blessing the Sick among Mormon Women," in D. Michael Quinn, ed., *The New Mormon History: Revisionist Essays on the Past* (Salt Lake City, UT: Signature Books, 1994).

New York Times. Cf. endnotes for specific dates and references.

Nichols, Jeffrey. *Prostitution, Politics, and Power: Salt Lake City, 1847–1918* (Urbana and Chicago: University of Illinois Press, 2002).

Noall, Claire. *Guardians of the Hearth* (Bountiful, UT: Horizon, 1974).

———. "Medicine among the Early Mormons," *Western Folklore Quarterly,* v. 18 (April 1953).

———. "Superstitions, Customs, and Prescriptions of Mormon Midwives," *California Folklore Quarterly,* v. 3, no. 2 (April 1944).

———. "Utah's Pioneer Women Doctors: The Story of Deseret Hospital," *Improvement Era* v. 42 (May 1939).

Ostling, Richard N., and Joan K. Ostling. *Mormon America: The Power and the Promise* (New York: HarperCollins, 1999).

Ponder, Kent. "Mormon Women, Prozac, and Therapy" (2003) (http://packham.n4m.org/prozac.htm).

Powell, Allen Kent. *Utah History Encyclopedia* (Salt Lake City, UT: University of Utah Press, 1994).

Quinn, D. Michael. "LDS Church Authority and New Plural Marriages, 1890–1904," *Dialogue: A Journal of Mormon Thought* (Spring 1985).

———. *The Mormon Hierarchy, 1832–1932: An American Elite* (New Haven, CT: Yale University Press, 1976).

———. *The Mormon Hierarchy: Extensions of Power* (Salt Lake City, UT: Signature Books, 1997). Cf. Chronological list of Mormon history from this book.

———. *The Mormon Hierarchy: Origins of Power* (Salt Lake City, UT: Signature Books, 1994).

———, ed., *The New Mormon History: Revisionist Essays on the Past* (Salt Lake City, UT: Signature Books, 1992).

Reynolds vs. United States. 98 US 145 (1878).

Richards, Ralph T. *Of Medicine, Hospitals, and Doctors* (Salt Lake City: University of Utah Press, 1953).

Rose, Blanche E. "Early Mormon Medical Practice," *Utah Historical Quarterly,* v. 10 (1942).

Salt Lake Herald. Cf. endnotes for specific dates and references.

Salt Lake Tribune. Cf. endnotes for specific dates and references.

Scott, Patricia L., and Linda Thatcher, eds. *Women in Utah History: Paradigm or Paradox?* (Logan, UT: Utah State University Press, 2005).

———. *Women in Utah History: Paradigm or Paradox?* (Logan, UT: Utah State University Press, 2005).

Seifrit, William. "The Prison Experience of Abraham H. Cannon," *Utah Historical Quarterly,* v. 53, no. 3. (Summer 1895)

Shannon, David A., ed. *Beatrice Potter Webb's American Diary, 1898* (Madison: University of Wisconsin Press, 1963).

Sheldon, Carrel Hilton. "Mormon Haters," in Claudia Bushman, ed., *Mormon Sisters: Women in Early Utah* (Logan, UT: Utah State University Press, 1997, p. 113).

Slaughter, William W. *Life in Zion: An Intimate Look at the Latter-day Saints, 1820–1995* (Salt Lake City, UT: Deseret Book Co., 1995).

Smith, Barbara B., and Blythe Thatcher, eds. *Heroines of the Restoration* (Salt Lake City, UT: Bookcraft, 1997).

Smith-Rosenberg, Carroll. *Disorderly Conduct: Visions of Gender in Victorian America* (London: Oxford University Press, 1986).

Stack, Peggy Fletcher. "Where Have All the Mormon Feminists Gone?" *Salt Lake Tribune* (www.beliefnet.com/story135_1356).

Stegner, Wallace. *The Mormons* (New York: Penguin, 1942).

Stenhouse, Fanny W. *Tell It All: The Tyranny of Mormonism, or, An English-woman in Utah* (London: Praeger Press, 1971).

Stone, Ann Gardner. "Dr. Ellen Brooke Ferguson: Nineteenth-Century Renaissance Woman," in Vicky Burgess-Olsen, ed., *Sister Saints* (Provo, UT: Brigham Young University Press, 1978).

Studt, Ward, MD, et al. *Medicine in the Intermountain West* (Salt Lake City, UT: Olympus Publishing Co., 1976).

Terry, Keith Calvin. "The Contributions of Medical Women during the First Fifty Years in Utah." Unpublished MA thesis (Brigham Young University, 1964).

Toscano, Margaret Merrill. "Is There a Place for Heavenly Mother in Mormon Theology: An Investigation into Discourses of Power" (www.affirmation.org/learning/is_there_a_place.shtml).

Twain, Mark. *Roughing It* (Hartford, CT: American Publishing Co., 1872).

University of California, Los Angeles. Medical Department. "Report to the President of the University," W. Jarvis Barlow, dean (July 1, 1912).

U.S. Census, 1910, 1920, 1930.

U.S. Congress. Hearing on Joint Resolution 68. February 15, 1898.

U.S. Senate. Proceedings Before the Committee on Privileges and Elections of the United States. April 21, 1904.

Utah, State of. *Laws of Utah, 1897*. CH. X, 24-25.

Utah, State of. *Public Documents,* 1897–98, Sec. 22. "Report of the Board of Health."

Utah, State of. *Public Documents,* 1899–1900, Sec. 22. "Report of the Board of Health."

Utah, State of. *Revised Statutes, 1898*. Title 24, 315–18.

Van Wagoner, Richard S. *Mormon Polygamy: A History* (Salt Lake City, UT: Signature Books, 1989).

Wallace, Irving. *The Twenty-seventh Wife* (New York: Simon and Schuster, 1961).

Walsh, Mary R. *Doctors Wanted: No Women Need Apply* (New Haven and London: Yale University Press, 1977).

Waters, Christine C. "Pioneering Women Physicians." John Sillito, ed. "From College to Market, the Professionalization of Women's Sphere." Papers presented at the Third Annual Meeting of the Utah Women's Association (Salt Lake City, 1983).

Wave. "Utah Women in Politics: The Balance of Power Held by the Fair Sex in the New State." San Francisco, January 17, 1897 (in Utah Historical Society).

Wells, Emmeline. Diary, v. 31 (February, 1905). At Brigham Young University, Provo, Utah.

———. "The History of Woman Suffrage in Utah: 1870–1900," in Carol Cornwall Madsen, ed., *Battle for the Ballot* (Logan, UT: Utah State University Press, 1997).

White, Jean Bickmore. "Dr. Martha Hughes Cannon: Doctor, Wife, Legislator, Exile," in Vicky Burgess-Olsen, ed., *Sister Saints* (Provo, UT: Brigham Young University Press, 1978).

———. "Woman's Place is in the Constitution," in C. Madsen, ed., *Battle for the Ballot* (Logan, UT: Utah State University Press, 1997).

Women's Exponent, The. Cf. endnotes for specific dates and references.

Wright, Robert. *The Moral Animal* (New York: Vintage, 1994).

Index

About the Author

Mari Graña left a career as an urban planner in California in 1988 and moved to New Mexico to begin a writing career. Her book on New Mexico regional history, *Begoso Cabin*, won the 2000 Willa Cather Award from Women Writing the West. She is also the author of the TwoDot book *Pioneer Doctor: The Story of a Woman's Work*, a biographical story of her grandmother, pioneering physician Mary Babcock Atwater. Mari lives in Santa Fe.